KITES FOR KIDS

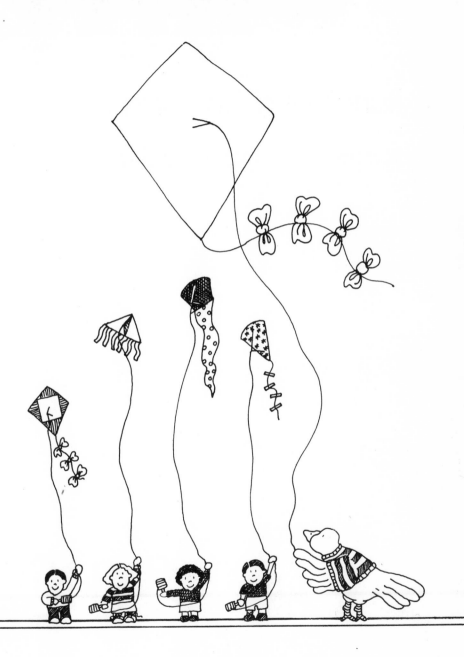

KITES

Burton and Rita Marks

illustrated by Lisa Campbell Ernst

Lothrop, Lee & Shepard Books
New York

FOR KIDS

Library of Congress Cataloging in Publication Data
Marks, Burton.
Kites for kids.
Includes index.
SUMMARY: Directions for making and flying a variety of simple kites.   1. Kites—Juve-
nile literature.   2. Kites—United States—Equipment and supplies—Directories—Juvenile
literature.   [1. Kites]   I. Marks, Rita, joint author.   II. Ernst, Lisa Campbell.   III. Title.
GV767.M37   796.1'5   79-22559
ISBN-0-688-41930-5
ISBN 0-688-51930-X lib. bdg.

For our parents—
with love

We would like to thank Judy Neuger, owner of the Kite Kompany in Chagrin Falls, Ohio, for her helpful suggestions and ideas and for allowing us to peruse her superb library of kite books, clippings, and memorabilia; thanks, also, to our sons, Craig and Wayne, who helped out in so many different ways; and finally we would like to express our gratitude and appreciation to Sharon Steinhoff of Lothrop, Lee & Shepard Books, for her invaluable advice and editorial assistance.

CONTENTS

KITES FOR KIDS

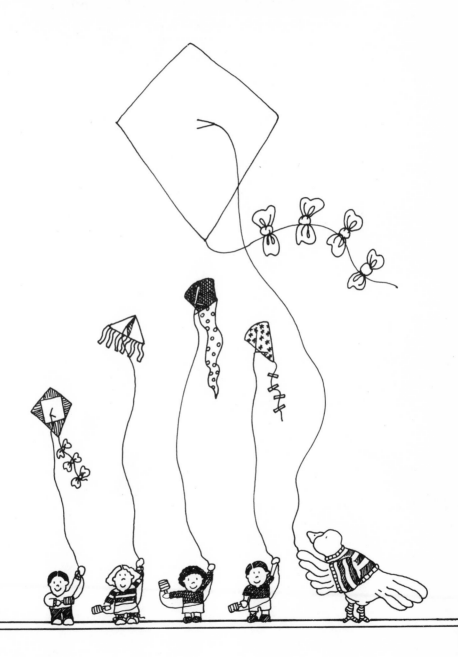

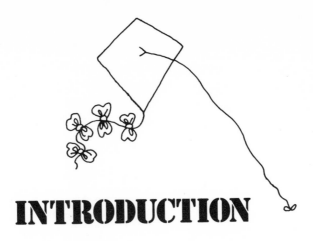

INTRODUCTION

On bright clear days when the wind is high, have you ever noticed that the sky is often dotted with colorful rocket ships and flying saucers—even dragons with long flowing tails? Of course, they are not really rocket ships or flying saucers or dragons—they are kites, soaring through the air at the end of a string. And down below each kite is a skillful navigator, someone just like you, whose steady hand is guiding the kite, "telling" it what to do and how to fly.

In this book you will find instructions for making and flying your own spaceships and fire-breathing monsters, plus a gallery of other fabulous kites. Each has been designed so that it is easy to build and easy to fly. And, best of all, these kites can be made with materials that you probably have on hand or that you can buy at very low cost.

You will also find simple directions for making kite tails, streamers, tassels, and reels, plus tips on kite safety, choosing a flying field, and estimating wind speeds—in fact, almost everything you'd want to know about making and flying kites.

Now turn the page, read on, and let the fun begin!

GETTING ACQUAINTED

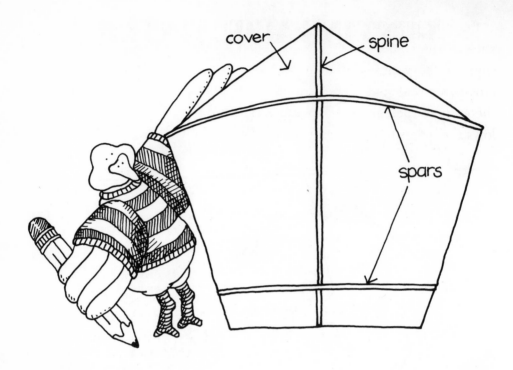

Before you start building and flying, it is a good idea to become familiar with the basic parts of the kite. Avoid confusion and disappointment later by looking over the diagrams and definitions in this chapter, then refer back to them if you need to.

COVER AND FRAME

The *cover* is the material that shapes the kite and provides the overall surface that catches the wind. In this book, covers are made from either paper or plastic. The painted or otherwise decorated side of the cover is called the front or *face*. The cover must be symmetrical—both halves identical—in order for the kite to fly. The halves of the cover are called *wings*.

Framing sticks support the cover and give it shape. The upright stick in the center of the kite is called the *spine*. The sticks that support the wings are called *spars*. The *spreader bar* is a rigid crosspiece that may also be used to support the wings, but only the ends of the spreader bar are connected to the cover. This allows the wings to move in flight, adjusting to changes in the wind.

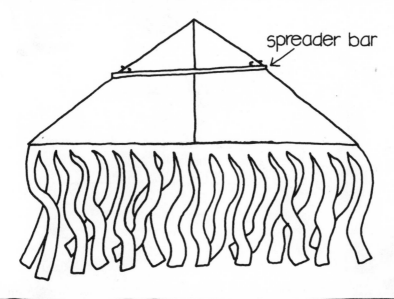

spreader bar

AMAZING MOMENTS IN KITE HISTORY

The largest kite in the world is flown each year in Hoshubana, Japan, a small village near Tokyo. It is thirty-six feet wide and forty-eight feet long—almost as large as a regulation tennis court. Weighing nearly a ton, this paper-and-bamboo giant has two hundred bridle lines, each one as thick as a broomstick. Depending upon the wind, fifty or more men are needed to send the kite aloft.

FLYING LINE

The kite flies at the end of a line called the *flying line*. The flying line steers the kite and holds it steady so that it can face the wind.

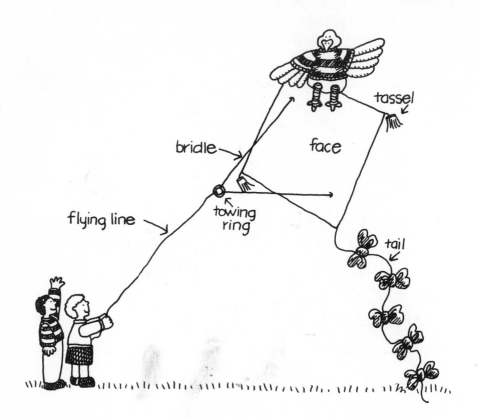

BRIDLE AND TOWING RING

The *bridle* is a bowed cord (or cords) that projects from the face of the kite. The purpose of the bridle is to hold the kite at the proper angle to the wind. The bridle lines are called *legs* and vary from two or more, depending upon the size and shape of the kite. Not all kites need a bridle, but most flat kites, like the Octopus on pages 97-99 and the Arch-top on pages 50-53, cannot be flown without them.

18

A small plastic ring, called a *towing ring*, links the bridle with the flying line. Since its position determines the angle at which the kite will fly, the towing ring is fastened to the bridle in such a way that it can be moved if necessary.

KEEL

Instead of a bridle and towing ring, many kites have a finlike projection called a *keel,* to which the flying line is directly attached.

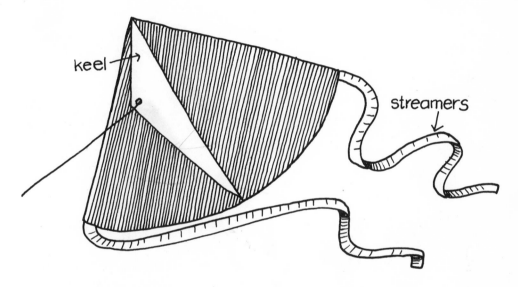

The main purpose of the keel is to steady the kite and guide it into the wind. A keel kite, such as the Star Ship on pages 68-72, is very easy to fly.

TAIL

Many kites can fly without a *tail,* but some need the extra drag, or wind resistance, that a tail provides to keep them steady and facing in the right direction. The type and length of kite tails vary from kite to kite and depend upon wind conditions, but the five easy kite tails described in this book can be adapted for nearly any kite you make.

Besides kite tails, *tassels* and *streamers* are used to provide additional flying stability. Instructions for making these are also included in chapter three.

AMAZING MOMENTS IN KITE HISTORY

In 1969, a group of high school students from Gary, Indiana, flew a train, or series, of nineteen kites to an altitude of 35,530 feet—about six and three-quarter miles up. The flight took over seven hours and required ten miles of flying line.

In 1979, Steve Flack, a seventeen-year-old student from Utica, New York, lofted a train of seven kites to a record altitude of 37,908 feet—over seven miles above the ground!

WHAT YOU NEED

Everything you need for making the kites in this book is easy to find and costs very little—sometimes nothing at all. Most of the tools and materials can be found around the house.

COVER MATERIALS

PAPER—Choose a strong lightweight paper, such as brown wrapping paper, butcher paper, or gift wrapping (even newspaper will do in a pinch). The largest sheet of paper you'll need is 24 × 30 inches, but this can be made from smaller pieces taped together if necessary. For some kites you'll need large lightweight paper bags, the kind you get in variety and department stores. (Do not use grocery bags. They are too small and too heavy.)

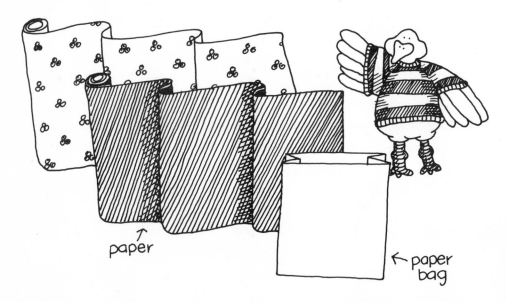

paper

← paper bag

PLASTIC—For plastic covers, use ordinary plastic trash bags or trash can liners. They are available at most supermarkets and hardware stores. You will also need these bags for making tails and plastic streamers.

dowel

FRAMING STICKS

The best framing sticks for the kites in this book are thin wooden dowels ⅛ inch in diameter. You can buy them in craft and hobby shops and some hardware stores. They are sold in 3-foot lengths and look like long sucker sticks.

Matchstick bamboo can be used instead of wooden dowels, but it may be more difficult to find. Your best source of supply is an old (or new) bamboo window shade. If you're lucky, you may find an old one in the garage or the attic that you can take apart. A new shade can be purchased at import shops and some department stores. Although it may seem rather expensive (about seven dollars), one 3-foot-wide shade will provide enough sticks for dozens of kites.

Although bamboo sticks are good substitutes for wooden dowels, they do have some drawbacks. Not only do they vary in size and quality, but they are also more flexible than wooden dowels and therefore may bow in flight. For best results, choose only round firm sticks. For spines and spreader bars, tape two sticks together, as shown, for added strength.

CAUTION: Bamboo sticks are not as smooth as dowels, so watch for splinters. To prevent mishaps, sand the sticks lightly with fine or medium sandpaper before using them.

matchstick bamboo shade →

← taped bamboo sticks

If neither wooden dowels nor bamboo sticks are readily available, try using dried plant stalks to frame your kites. Many dried weeds and flower stems are lightweight, yet surprisingly strong, making them ideal for kite-building. If you scout an open field, a garden, or a vacant lot, you should find enough good sticks to get you started. Pick them in the spring as soon as the weather is dry.

Look for tall, straight sticks, between 2 and 3 feet long, that are not too brittle. Cut off the top growth, then sand the sides with medium sandpaper until they are smooth and even.

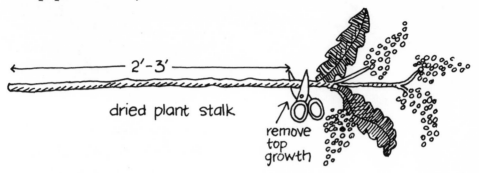

2'–3'

dried plant stalk

remove
top
growth

FLYING LINE

The flying line should be strong, lightweight, and easy to handle. A length of 300 feet is all you'll need. The best line for the kites in this book is ordinary lightweight cotton twine. If braided fishing line is handy, it's another good choice, but be sure it's a light color. See-through plastic lines and dark-colored lines (of any kind) "disappear" on the ground and become hopelessly snarled. Don't use sewing thread for a flying line either since it's hard to wind and tangles easily. It cuts your fingers too.

BRIDLE CORD AND TOWING RING

The ideal cord to use for the bridle is #18 braided nylon twine. It is smooth and silky, which allows the towing ring to be moved easily. Look for nylon twine in hardware and variety stores. A small 100-foot spool is more than enough. If nylon twine is not available, you can use flying line string.

For the towing ring, use a small plastic curtain ring. You can buy these rings in variety stores, craft centers, or wherever drapery accessories are sold.

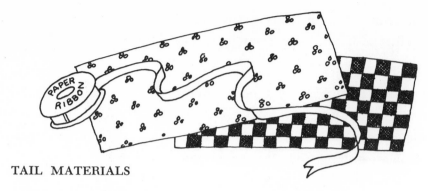

TAIL MATERIALS

Kite tails can be made from scraps of plastic, paper, or cloth—whatever is handy. You will also need a spool of ¾-inch paper ribbon and several feet of household string.

COVER DECORATING MATERIALS

You can decorate your paper kites with poster or acrylic paints, felt markers, colored pencils, watercolors, colored inks, or crayons. For plastic kites, use acrylic paints, crayons, or permanent felt markers. Glitter and shiny gift wrapping will also be useful if you have them.

TAPE

You'll need a roll of cellophane tape or package sealing tape (or both) for securing the framing sticks, reinforcing edges, and making general repairs. If the tape is going to show, cellophane is the better choice. Cloth tape (such as Mystik cloth tape or duct tape) is suggested where a stronger bond is needed. You can purchase these tapes in hardware and variety stores.

GLUE

Use an all-purpose white glue, such as Sobo or Elmer's Glue-All, which is available from hardware stores and craft centers. For the Spinner Reel (pages 38-39), you will need model-making glue (such as Duco Cement).

TOOLS

No special tools are required, but you should have a pair of scissors, a pencil, a felt-tip pen or crayon (for marking on plastic), a stapler, and a long measuring stick—either a yardstick or a meter stick. For the Spinner Reel, you will need a hammer and a small nail. A nail or sharp-pointed pencil will also come in handy for poking tying holes in paper and plastic covers.

← pin-on drapery
hook

MISCELLANEOUS SUPPLIES

With these few household items, your roundup of supplies will be complete: 1⅜-inch pin-on drapery hooks, notebook paper reinforcement rings (Dennison self-sticking pres-a-ply work well on both paper and plastic), a bobby pin, and a large safety pin. A can (cardboard or tin) with a plastic lid, a round oatmeal box, and a ⅝-inch wooden dowel will also be needed to make the reels.

CONSTRUCTION TIPS
AND TECHNIQUES

The kites in this book differ not only in appearance but in the number of their parts as well. However, many of the construction techniques, such as attaching the framing sticks and reinforcing the cover, are the same for each. These basic methods are described step-by-step in this chapter and indicated with an asterisk (*) in each project. Also included here are a few simple procedures that will help to make your kite-making easier and more fun.

GETTING READY

Before you start to build, gather all your materials to make sure you have everything you need. Read through the instructions carefully. Then follow each step, one at a time.

Clear a large flat surface to work on. Two card tables placed side by side will do nicely. If you plan to use paint, glue, or glitter, protect your work surface by spreading out newspapers first.

MEASURING

To make sure your projects get off the ground, measure carefully and accurately with a yardstick (or a meter stick). Never guess at a measurement or make up one of your own.

The measurements for each kite are given in inches and feet. If you use the metric system, there is a conversion table on page 125 that lists metric equivalents for all the measurements in this book.

HOW TO ATTACH THE FRAMING STICKS

To fasten a spine or spar to the back of the kite cover, use strips of cellophane tape or package sealing tape. Lay the tape at right angles to the stick, as shown, and press firmly. At the tips of the stick, however, the tape should run lengthwise, overlapping to the front of the cover.

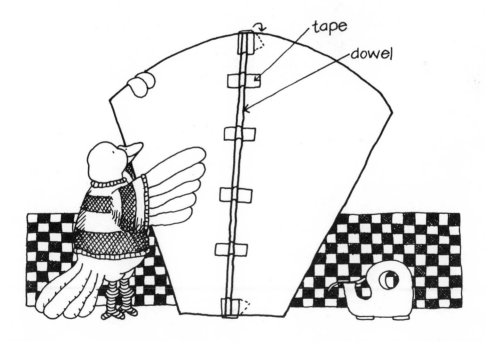

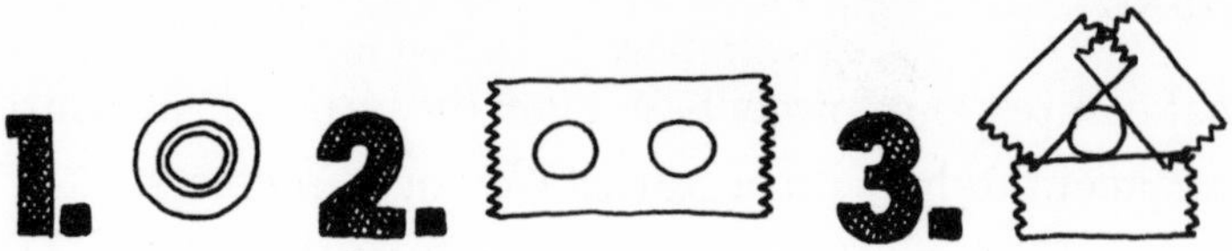

HOW TO REINFORCE THE COVER

Whenever a hole is punched in the cover (for attaching a bridle, a spreader bar, and so on), it must be reinforced to prevent tears. There are three ways that you can do this:

1. Circle the holes with cloth reinforcement rings (see page 28).
2. Place cellophane tape over the points to be punched. Then, with a nail or a sharp-pointed pencil, poke the holes through the tape and the cover.
3. Surround the holes with small pieces of cellophane tape as shown.

HOW TO ATTACH THE BRIDLE AND THE TOWING RING

A simple two-legged bridle that fastens to the spine is all you'll need for the kites in this book. Here's how to attach it to the kite cover and frame:

1. From the back or dowel-side of the kite, use a nail or a sharp-pointed pencil to poke holes in the cover at the tying points as shown in the diagram.
2. Reinforce the holes with tape or cloth rings (see page 28).
3. Cut the bridle cord to the length given in the list of materials for the kite you are making.
4. Turn the cover over. Run one end of the bridle cord through one hole, under the dowel (or dowels), and out the opposite hole. (This is easier to do if you first loop the cord through a

bobby pin as shown, using the pin like a needle.) Knot securely in the front. Thread the opposite end of the cord through the remaining holes in the same way.

Attaching the Bridle

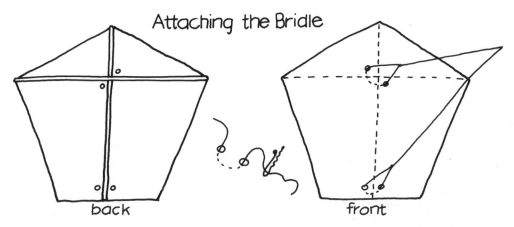

back   front

Now you are ready to attach the towing ring to the bridle cord. The position of the ring will vary depending upon the strength of the wind. For normal wind conditions (see page 105), fasten the ring so it is about one quarter of the way down the face of the kite when the bridle is pulled taut (Figure 1). In strong winds, it should be moved up a little (Figure 2); in light winds, move it slightly closer to the midpoint (Figure 3). The correct position can only be determined by trial and error. But with a little practice, you will be able to do this easily.

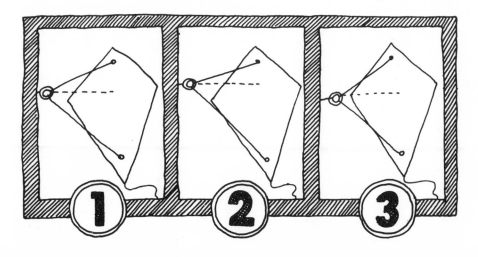

TO ATTACH THE TOWING RING:

1. Form a small loop in the cord where the towing ring is to be attached.
2. Bring this loop through the ring.
3. Pull the loop back over the top and sides of the ring.
4. Pull the bridle legs and ring in opposite directions until a firm knot is formed.

TO MOVE THE TOWING RING:

1. Loosen the knot by pulling on the loop at the bottom.
2. Slide the ring to its new position and tighten the cord around it as before.

HOW TO ATTACH THE FLYING LINE

One of the simplest ways of attaching the flying line to the kite is to fasten a safety pin to the end of the line and to pin the line to the towing ring or the keel. This will also allow you to switch the line easily from one kite to another.

Use a safety pin that is at least 1½ inches long. Run one end of the line through the opening in the head of the pin and tie securely. Attach the pin as shown.

If a safety pin is not available, simply knot the end of the line to the towing ring or to the tip of the keel.

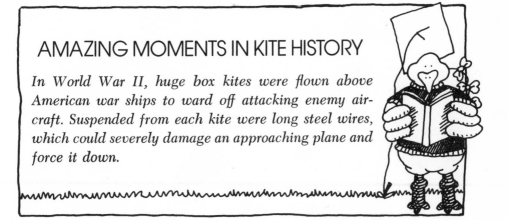

AMAZING MOMENTS IN KITE HISTORY

In World War II, huge box kites were flown above American war ships to ward off attacking enemy aircraft. Suspended from each kite were long steel wires, which could severely damage an approaching plane and force it down.

A kite tail is important for two reasons: it stabilizes, or steadies, the kite, and it keeps the kite facing in the right direction. A good tail should not be too heavy. It is the length and the design of a tail that produce its drag, not the weight. The length of your kite's tail should vary according to the strength of the wind. For normal winds, use a tail that is four times longer than the spine. Then add to it when the winds are strong. In light gentle winds, it may be necessary to shorten the tail just a little. The following five tails can be fastened to the spine with cellophane or package sealing tape.

BOW TIES—Cut tissue paper or paper napkins into 6-inch squares. Pinch each square in the center and twist it like a bow. Staple the bows at 8-inch intervals along a narrow plastic streamer or paper ribbon.

STRIP TAIL—Cut a plastic trash bag or freezer bag into strips 2 inches wide and 14 inches long. Tie the strips together, end to end, with large bold knots.

FLAGSHIP TAIL—Cut flags from sheets of typing paper, cutting five flags from each sheet as shown. Decorate with crayons, paint, or felt markers. Staple the flags at 3-inch intervals along a paper ribbon or a narrow plastic streamer.

BUTTERFLY TAIL—Cut strips 2 inches wide and 10 inches long from crepe paper, cloth, or plastic. Knot the strips at 6- to 8-inch intervals around a string, plastic streamer, or paper ribbon. Wrap tape just below each "butterfly" strip to hold it in place.

FIRECRACKERS—From typing paper or gift wrapping, cut strips 1 inch wide and 6 inches long. Staple the strips 4 inches apart along a paper ribbon as shown.

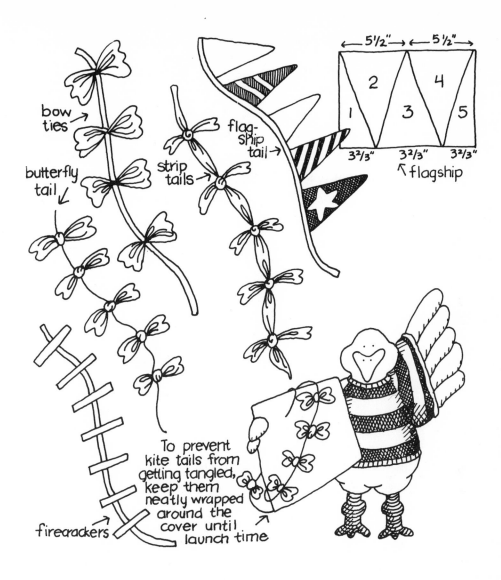

bow
ties →

butterfly
tail ↙

strip
tails →

flag-
ship
tail →

↖ flagship

← 5½″ → ← 5½″ →

| | 2 | | 4 | |
|1| | 3 | | 5|

3²/₃″   3²/₃″   3²/₃″

To prevent
kite tails from
getting tangled,
keep them
neatly wrapped
around the
cover until
launch time

firecrackers →

TWO SIMPLE REELS

To fly a kite you'll only need one piece of special equipment—a
reel to hold the flying line. A good reel makes it easier to wind
and unwind the line and also helps to keep the line from getting
tangled. Although some fliers like to use an ordinary fishing reel,
these can jam easily if you're not careful. Reels without moving

parts, like the easy-to-make Spinner Reel and Instant Reel, are more reliable and in many ways easier to use.

SPINNER REEL

YOU WILL NEED:

a can with a plastic lid (a lightweight powdered drink can is ideal)
a wooden dowel, about ⅝ inch in diameter and 6 inches longer
   than the can
small nail with head, about ¾ inch long
model-making glue (such as Duco Cement)
sharp-pointed scissors, hammer
flying line

WHAT TO DO:

1. Remove the plastic lid from the can. With the scissors, cut a hole the same diameter as the dowel in the center of the lid. Replace the lid.
2. Turn the can upside down. Using the hammer and nail, punch a hole in the bottom of the can, exactly in the center. Remove the nail.

3. Put glue on one end of the dowel. Push the dowel (glued-end first) through the hole in the lid until it touches the hole in the bottom of the can.

4. Drive the small nail through the hole in the can and into the dowel. Let the glue dry overnight.

5. Tie the end of the flying line tightly around the center of the can. (This will prevent the line from running out and slipping off the reel.) Then wind the remainder of the line onto the reel.

6. To operate the reel, hold the dowel in one hand and wind the line with the other. To feed out line, let the dowel turn freely in your hand as shown.

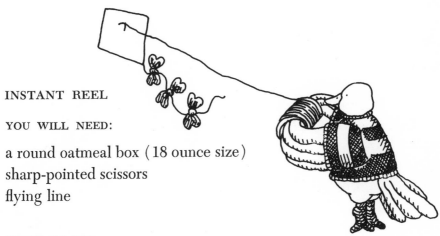

INSTANT REEL

YOU WILL NEED:

a round oatmeal box (18 ounce size)
sharp-pointed scissors
flying line

WHAT TO DO:

This is one of the easiest of all reels to make, but also one of the best. Simply remove the lid from the box; then, with the scissors, cut away the bottom of the box, forming a tube. To complete the reel, wind on the flying line, first tying the end securely around the box.

To operate the reel, hold it in one hand and wind the line with the other. To feed out line, hold your fingers or hands inside the reel like a muff and let the reel revolve around them.

PAPER TASSELS

Paper tassels are easy and fun to make. Use them to dress up flat kites like the Arch-top and the Japanese Fighting Kite. Or make extra-large tassels and tie them to the end of a tail.

YOU WILL NEED:

tissue paper
tape, string, scissors

WHAT TO DO:

1. For each tassel, cut a sheet of paper 8 inches square and fold it in half.
2. Cut fringe along the side opposite the fold, leaving about ½ inch uncut near the fold edge.
3. Tie a string loosely around the center of the fold.
4. Tightly roll the paper from one short side to the other and tape closed at the uncut end.

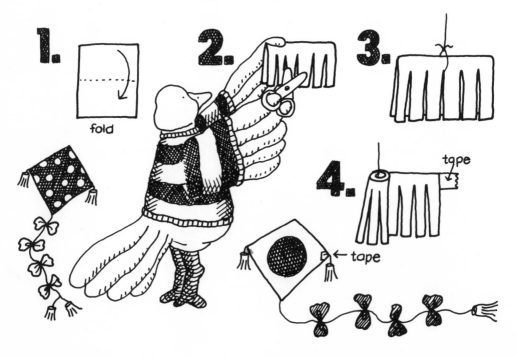

PLASTIC STREAMERS

Streamers can be made quickly and easily from a plastic trash bag. This is how to do it: Fold the bag in half from top to bottom. Then fold it in half again the same way. Cut narrow strips about 1½ inches wide, as shown, and unfold. For longer streamers, tape two or three strips together end to end.

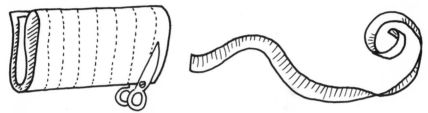

DECORATING YOUR KITE

One of the best things about building your own kite is that you can decorate it any way you want. It's fun knowing that no other kite will be exactly like yours. The cover ideas described at the end of each project will get you started, but don't stop there. Use your imagination to create some unique designs of your own.

For best results, plan your design carefully before you begin. Sketch it lightly with a pencil or felt-tip pen; then fill in the solid blocks of color, saving the details for last.

Remember that your kite will usually be seen from far away, so keep your design simple and use only bright, clear colors. A kite with only two or three colors is often more eye-catching than a fancy, multi-colored design. If you use bold black outlines, your colors will stand out and appear to be brighter.

It is a good idea to decorate the kite cover before attaching the framing dowels, especially if you are using crayons or colored pencils. Be sure to decorate only the front, or face, of the kite. This is the side everyone will see when your kite is flying overhead.

When you are choosing your decorating materials, it is best to avoid using any type of decoration that will add to the weight of your kite. The lighter the cover, the better your kite will fly. Here are a few more helpful decorating tips:

- Thin your paints with a little water before using them and apply only one coat. Paint that is too thick might crack or peel. It can also add unnecessary weight to the cover.

- For plastic covers, use only white plastic if you plan to decorate the kite. Dark-colored plastic is difficult to decorate, even with acrylic paint.

- Use only permanent (not water-base) felt markers on a plastic cover. Look for the words *permanent* or *waterproof* on the label.

- If you decorate with paints or colored inks, allow the cover to dry thoroughly before proceeding with the kite construction. Paper covers may take an hour or more to dry. Plastic covers dry quickly—in about twenty minutes.

- To cover newsprint easily, apply a thin coat of ordinary white latex paint, the kind used for painting interior walls. When the paint is dry, color the paper with crayons or felt markers.

AMAZING MOMENTS IN KITE HISTORY

In 1749, two Scottish scientists, Alexander Wilson and Thomas Melville, fastened thermometers to kites in order to record the temperature of the air at high altitudes. This was the first recorded attempt to obtain scientific data using kites.

· For an unusual effect, decorate your covers with gold or silver glitter. If you are using paint, sprinkle glitter over the paint while it is still wet. Let the paint dry, then shake off any glitter that doesn't stick. If you are not using paint, spread a thin layer of white glue over the areas you want to decorate. Then dust glitter lightly over the glue. Be sure to do this over newspaper or other protective covering—it can be very messy!

· Use a fairly wide brush for painting large areas and a smaller brush for details. To keep your kite design bright and sharp, wash your brushes thoroughly before switching colors. And be sure that one color is dry before painting over it with another. When you are finished painting, wash all brushes in soap and water and lay them flat to dry.

And now that you know the basics, get set for some high-flying fun—it's time to build!

PARADE OF KITES

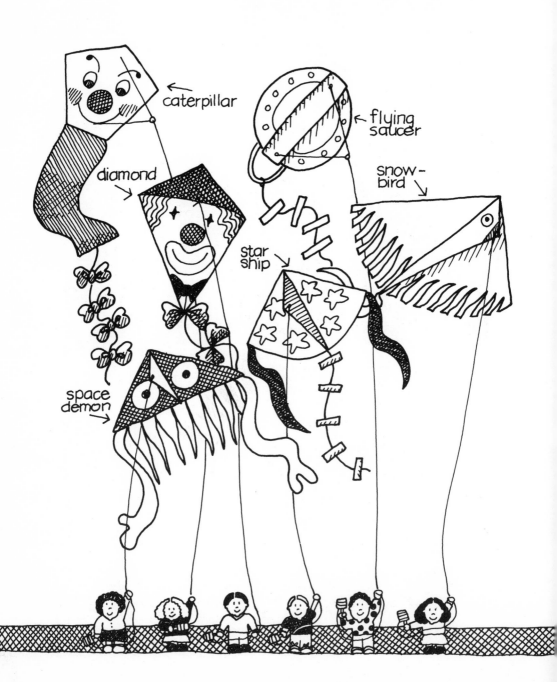

← arch-top

←delta

Japanese
fighter

octopus →

two-
stick

astro
glider

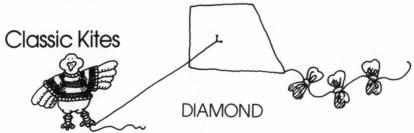

Classic Kites

DIAMOND

This familiar-looking kite is the one you see most often in picture books, toy shops, and neighborhood parks. It is regarded as a traditional American design, although diamond-shaped kites have been flown in Asian countries for hundreds of years.

If you have never made or flown a kite before, this is a good one to try first. Unlike other flat-surfaced kites, the Diamond does not require a bridle, making it a very easy kite to build and fly.

YOU WILL NEED:

sheet of strong lightweight paper, 23 inches wide and 30 inches long, for the cover
⅛-inch dowel, 30 inches long, for the spine
⅛-inch dowel, 23 inches long, for the spar
flying line
tail
cellophane tape or package sealing tape
reinforcement rings (optional)
scissors, pencil, measuring stick, decorating materials

WHAT TO DO:
* For steps marked with this symbol, refer to chapter three for detailed how-to instructions.

1. Fold the cover paper in half lengthwise. On the side opposite the fold, mark a point 8 inches from either short edge. From this point, use the measuring stick to draw straight lines to the opposite corners as shown.

46

2. Cut out the cover along these lines, cutting through both layers of paper at the same time. Open the cover and lay it flat. Decorate.

* 3. Turn the cover face down. Tape the spine to the center fold. Tape the spar between the tips of the wings.

* 4. With a pencil, poke tying holes where the spine and the spar cross as shown. Reinforce the holes with tape or cloth rings.

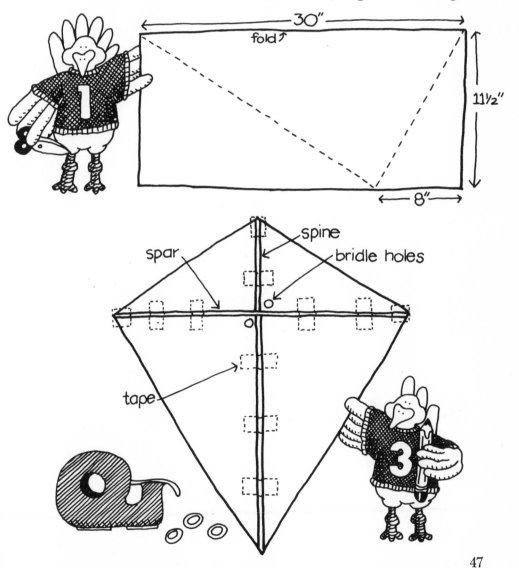

5. Turn the kite face up. Run the flying line through one hole, under the dowels, and out the other hole. (To make threading easier, use a bobby-pin needle as shown.) Knot the line securely in the front.
6. Choose a tail from those described in chapter three and tape it to the bottom of the spine.

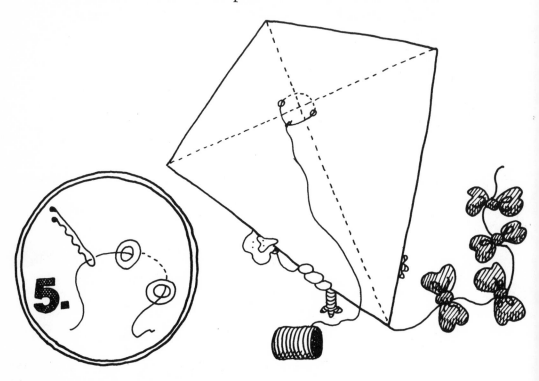

VARIATION: PLASTIC DIAMOND

This lightweight version of the Diamond kite is ideally suited for soft gentle winds. To make it, follow the directions for the Diamond kite, substituting plastic for the paper cover. Cut the plastic from a large trash bag, using a crayon or felt-tip pen to draw the cutting lines. You will also need a second spar 11 inches long to help support the cover. Tape it across the spine 11 inches up from the bottom of the kite as shown.

DECORATING TIPS: For the clown design, use a white paper or plastic cover and let the cover be the color of the face. Make the hair, nose, and mouth red. Draw large black eyes. Use any bright color for the hat and bow tie, such as yellow or green. Continue the bow tie theme by making a Bow Tie tail, using tissue paper bows that match the colors in the face.

Almost any design looks good on a Diamond kite. You might print your initials or your first name, if it is short enough. A cartoon hero or a favorite food is also an eye-catching subject.

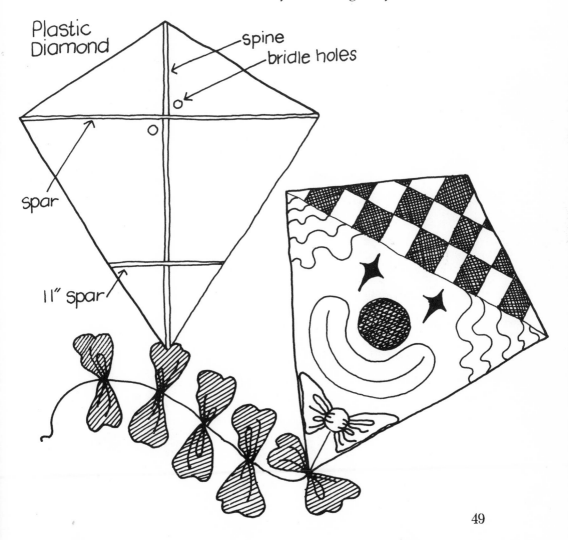

ARCH-TOP

In 1825, George Pocock, an English schoolmaster and part-time inventor, used two giant Arch-top kites to pull a carriage over a hundred miles across the British countryside. With four passengers aboard, the carriage reportedly reached speeds of up to twenty-five miles per hour. Since Pocock's incredible journey, inventive fliers have used kites to tow everything from sleds to small fishing boats.

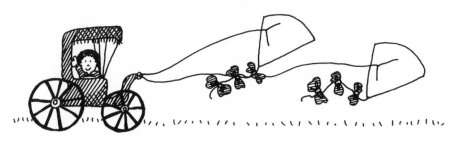

This simplified version of the Arch-top kite is not strong enough to tow a boat or even a sled, but it might pull a small wagon along a smooth path. Because of its unique design, the Arch-top is a fast, steady climber, performing best in light to moderate winds.

YOU WILL NEED:

sheet of strong lightweight paper, 22 inches wide and 25 inches
   long, for the cover
⅛-inch dowel, 25 inches long, for the spine
⅛-inch dowel, 25 inches long, for the spar. Do not substitute a
   dried plant stalk for this dowel, since it may snap when bowed.
flying line
33-inch bridle cord and towing ring
tail
cellophane tape or package sealing tape
reinforcement rings (optional)
scissors, pencil, measuring stick, decorating materials

WHAT TO DO:

* For steps marked with this symbol, refer to chapter three for detailed how-to instructions.

1. Fold the cover paper in half lengthwise. On the side opposite the fold, mark a point 6 inches from either end.

2. From this point, draw a curved line to the nearest opposite corner and a straight line to the other opposite corner as shown. Cut out the cover along these lines, cutting through both layers of paper at the same time.

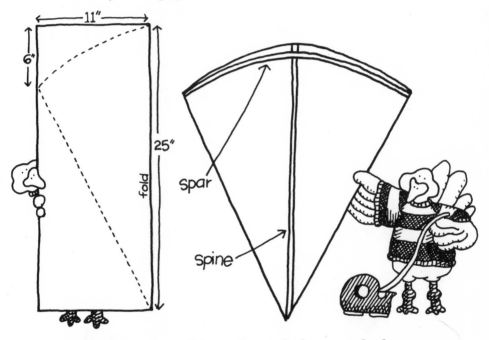

3. Open the cover and lay it flat with the curved edge pointing upward.

4. Decorate the cover.

* 5. Turn the cover face down. Tape the spine to the center fold.

6. Soak the spar in warm water for a few minutes to make it more flexible. Then wipe the spar with a cloth until it is thoroughly dry.

* 7. Tape the exact center of the spar to the spine ½ inch from

the top. Then bow the spar ends slightly and tape them to the tips of the wings, as shown, overlapping the tape to the front of the cover. Tape the remainder of the spar securely in place.

* 8. Poke holes for the bridle cord where the spine and the spar cross and at the opposite end of the spine 8 inches from the bottom. Reinforce with tape or cloth rings.

* 9. Turn the kite face up. Attach the bridle and the towing ring. Pin or tie on the flying line.

10. Choose a tail from those described in chapter three and tape it to the base of the spine.

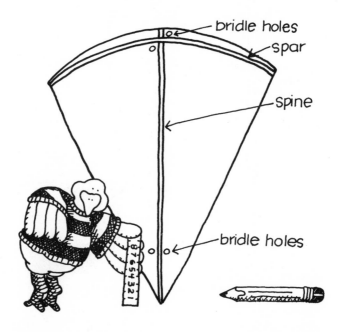

DECORATING TIPS: An owl design is easy to make if you use brown wrapping paper for the cover. Using the illustration as a guide, draw the feather markings directly on the cover with a dark brown crayon or felt marker. Paint the eyes yellow or white with bright green centers, or cut them from lightweight paper and glue in place. Color the beak and talons yellow or orange.

The shape of the Arch-top kite is perfect for a hot-air balloon design. Draw the balloon using two bright contrasting colors, such as red and yellow. Paint the basket brown and the background light blue or gray.

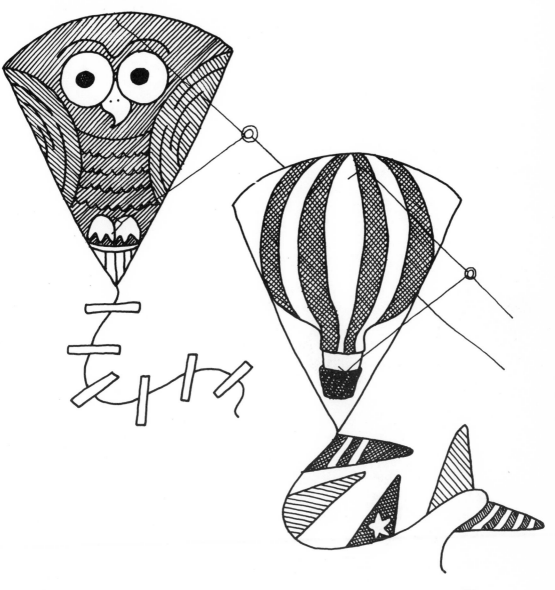

TWO-STICK

In the mid 1700s, Benjamin Franklin flew a kite in a thunderstorm to prove his theory that lightning was a form of electricity. For his experiment, Franklin used a simple Two-stick kite fashioned from a silk handkerchief with two cedar sticks tied to the corners.

Here is a modern version of the Two-stick kite made with wooden dowels and a plastic cover. It is one of the easiest of all kites to build and is light enough to launch in the gentlest summer breeze. But first one note of warning: Don't attempt Franklin's foolhardy experiment by flying this kite *or any kite* in an electrical storm. Franklin miraculously escaped injury, but he could have been killed by the very sparks of electricity that he discovered.

AMAZING MOMENTS IN KITE HISTORY

In 1847, a suspension bridge was built across the Niagara River with the aid of a kite. When chief engineer T. G. Hulett was unable to carry the first steel cables across the mighty Niagara Gorge, he decided that a kite might solve his problem. A kite-flying contest was held and Hulett offered ten dollars to anyone who could fly a kite line to the other side of the river. Only one flier was successful—a determined young boy named Homan Walsh. When Walsh's kite landed on the opposite shore, the flying line was then tied to stronger lines, which were used to pull the cables in place.

YOU WILL NEED:

plastic trash bag for the cover

two ⅛-inch dowels, each 21¼ inches long—one for the spine and one for the spar. If you substitute matchstick bamboo, be sure to use two sticks taped together for the spine (see page 24). This kite will loop and dive unless the spine is rigid.

flying line

29-inch bridle cord and towing ring

tail

2 narrow plastic streamers, each 3 feet long

cellophane tape or package sealing tape

reinforcement rings (optional)

scissors, measuring stick, crayon or felt-tip pen for marking on plastic, decorating materials

WHAT TO DO:

* For steps marked with this symbol, refer to chapter three for detailed how-to instructions.

1. From the plastic bag, cut a sheet 15 inches square for the cover. Decorate.

* 2. Turn the cover face down. Tape the spine and the spar between opposite corners as shown.

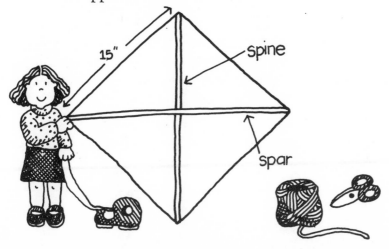

15"   spine

spar

3. Tape a plastic streamer to each end of the spar and a tail to the base of the spine.

* 4. Poke tying holes for the bridle on both sides of the spine 3 inches from the top and bottom. Reinforce the holes.

* 5. Turn the kite face up. Attach the bridle and the towing ring. Pin or tie on the flying line.

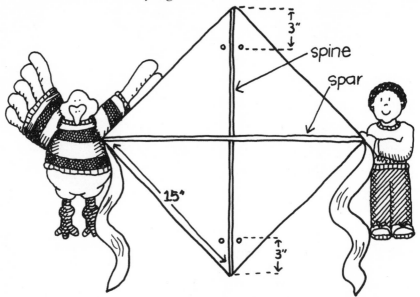

DECORATING TIPS: This is an exceptionally small kite, so be sure your design is bright and bold enough to be seen easily when it is high overhead.

To make a sun design, draw a circle in the center of the cover using a large paper plate as a guide. Then draw the sun's "rays" as shown in the illustration. Color the sun yellow or yellow-orange, adding details with black or brown. Color the background light blue.

Since the cover is square, why not try a geometric design? It can be as simple as a square within a square. Or draw lines connecting the opposite corners, then paint each section a contrasting color.

AMAZING MOMENTS IN KITE HISTORY

In 1901, Guglielmo Marconi, inventor of the wireless telegraph, used a kite to loft an antenna four hundred feet in order to receive the first radio signal ever transmitted across an ocean.

JAPANESE FIGHTING KITE

Kitefighting, as practiced by the Japanese, is a highly competitive and often dangerous sport. Before a battle, kite warriors coat their flying lines with glue and bits of powdered glass. Sometimes curved steel blades are fastened to the tails. The object of the fight is to entangle an opponent's line and cut it down. Once a kite has fallen, the victor claims it as his own.

The kite shown here is an adaptation of a popular Japanese fighting kite called a Nagasaki-hata. Like all fighting kites, the Nagasaki-hata is a strong and lively flier. The colorful tassels on each side of the kite help to steady its flight as well as add to its beauty.

YOU WILL NEED:

sheet of strong lightweight paper, 30 inches wide and 24 inches long, for the cover
⅛-inch dowel, 24 inches long, for the spine
⅛-inch dowel, 32 inches long, for the spar. Do not substitute a dried plant stalk for this dowel, since it may snap when bowed.
flying line
40-inch bridle cord and towing ring
tail
cellophane tape or package sealing tape
reinforcement rings (optional)
2 paper tassels (see chapter three)
scissors, pencil, measuring stick, decorating materials

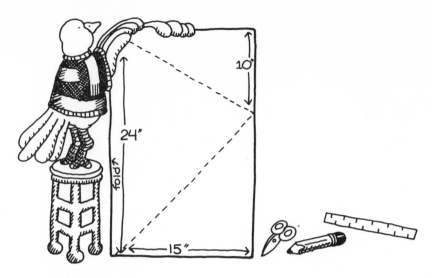

WHAT TO DO:

* For steps marked with this symbol, refer to chapter three for detailed how-to instructions.

1. Fold the cover paper in half, bringing the short sides together.
2. On the side opposite the fold, mark a point 10 inches from either end. From this point, draw straight lines to the opposite corners as shown.
3. Cut out the cover along these lines, cutting both halves together. Unfold the cover and lay it flat.
4. Decorate the cover.

AMAZING MOMENTS IN KITE HISTORY

The ancient Chinese believed that kites could ward off evil spirits. Even today in China the kite is regarded as a symbol of good luck.

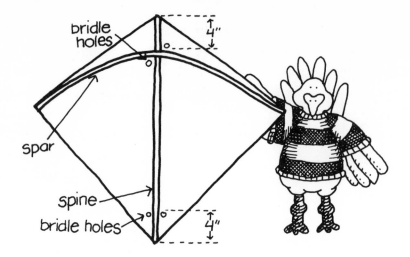

* 5. Turn the cover face down. Tape the spine to the center fold.
* 6. Bow the spar slightly and tape it between the tips of the wings as shown. The spar should cross the spine about 4 inches from the top. Tape the spar firmly in place, making sure that it curves evenly on both sides of the spine.
* 7. Poke holes for the bridle cord where the spine and the spar cross and at the opposite end of the spine 4 inches from the bottom. Reinforce the holes.
* 8. Turn the kite face up. Attach the bridle and the towing ring. Pin or tie on the flying line.
  9. Tape a tail to the base of the spine and paper tassels to the tips of the wings.

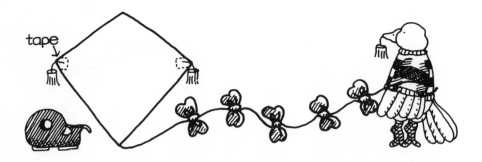

DECORATING TIPS: The traditional colors of the Nagasaki-hata are red, white, and blue. The designs are usually very simple, sometimes nothing more than three bold diagonal stripes. If you would like your kite to have an authentic Japanese look, try copying the design shown in the upper right illustration. The sun should be bright red against a white sky. Color the water dark blue.

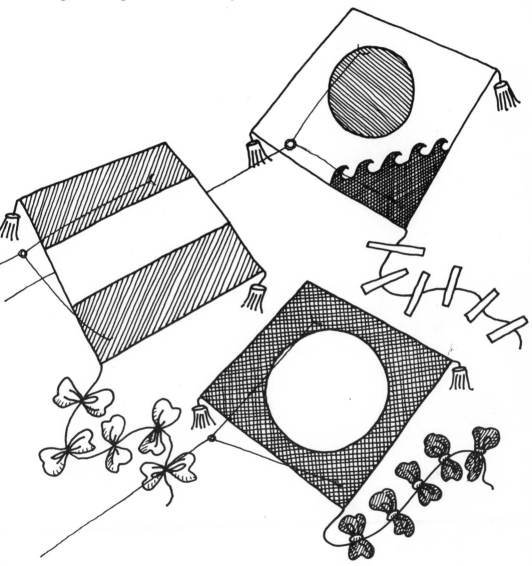

61

Space Cruisers

DELTA

The Delta is a relative newcomer to the kite world but it is fast becoming one of the most popular of all kites. Its basic shape is a triangle with two equal sides. A keel, which projects from the center of the triangle, acts as a rudder to guide the kite and hold it steady. The Delta is not a rigid kite—its wings move in flight, allowing it to adjust to varying winds.

YOU WILL NEED:

lightweight paper bag, at least 19 inches wide, for the cover and
    the keel
two ⅛-inch dowels, each 19 inches long, for the spars
⅛-inch dowel, 21 inches long, for the spreader bar
flying line
plastic trash bag
cloth tape (such as Mystik cloth tape or duct tape)
cellophane tape or package sealing tape
reinforcement rings (optional)
white glue
two 1⅜-inch pin-on drapery hooks
scissors, pencil, measuring stick, decorating materials

WHAT TO DO:
* For steps marked with this symbol, see chapter three for detailed how-to instructions.

1. Cut across the opening of the paper bag so the edges are straight and even. Lay the bag flat with the open end at the top.

2. From the upper left corner, measure and mark a point 19 inches across the top. From the same corner, measure and mark a point 16 inches down the left side. Draw a straight line connecting these two points.

3. Cut along this line, cutting both sides of the bag at the same time.

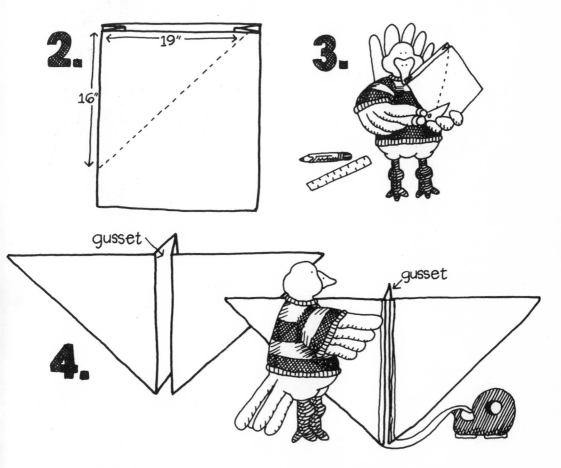

4. Open the cover. Note the gusset (folded side panel) in the center. Bring the fold edges of the wings together and tape the gusset closed. Turn the cover so that the long side is the bottom edge.

5. To make the keel, cut a rectangle 5 inches wide and 16 inches long from the unused portion of the bag or a separate sheet of strong lightweight paper. From either short side, measure over 7 inches and mark a point along the long edge. From this point, draw straight lines to the opposite corners as shown. Cut out the keel along these lines.

6. Lay the keel on one side of the gusset, making sure that the short side of the keel is pointed toward the top of the kite. Glue the keel in place.
7. Trim the gusset so that it is the same shape as the keel.
8. Decorate the cover and the keel.

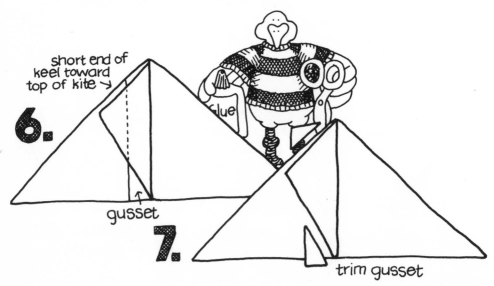

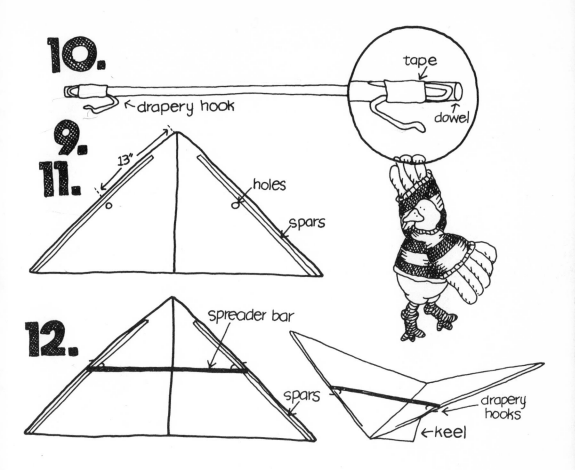

* 9. Turn the cover face down. Tape the spars ½ inch in from the leading edges of the wings and even with the bottom edge.

10. Using cloth tape, fasten a drapery hook to each end of the spreader bar as shown.

* 11. From the top of the kite, measure 13 inches down the side of each wing and poke a small hole beside the inside edges of the spars. Reinforce the holes with cloth rings or tape.

12. Lay the spreader bar across the wings and insert a drapery hook into each hole. The wings should form a slight V-shape when viewed head on.

13. Use the plastic trash bag to make the tail streamers. From a single layer of plastic, cut a rectangle 2 feet wide and 3 feet long. Tape one of the longer sides to the bottom edge of the kite. Then, starting at the opposite end, cut slits 1½ inches apart, leaving a short uncut border near the taped edge.

* 14. Reinforce the edges of the keel with tape, covering the double edges of the gusset at the same time. Poke a hole in the tip of the keel about ½ inch in from the edge as shown. Reinforce the hole and attach the flying line.

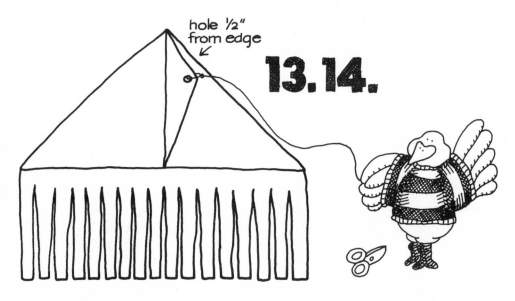

hole ½" from edge

13. 14.

DECORATING TIPS: One of the most effective ways of decorating a Delta kite is with two contrasting colors—one color for the wings, the other for the keel. Or use a different color for each of the wings and a third color for the keel. For variety, add stripes, stars, or geometric shapes.

The shape of the Delta kite suggests many other design ideas—spaceships, bats, stingrays, butterflies, airplanes, birds. . . . Let your imagination go!

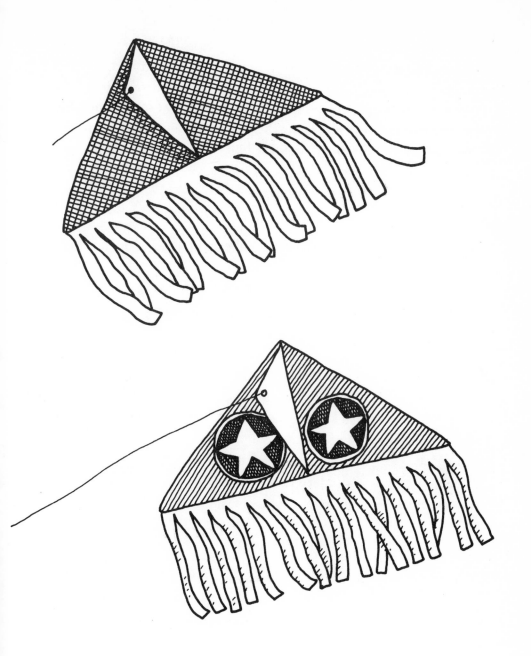

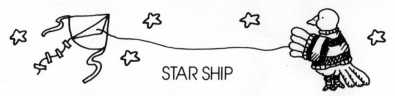

STAR SHIP

This is one of the easiest kites to fly. It will soar from your hand the instant it catches a breeze, then climb as high as the line will allow. Once you fly this delightful kite, it may well become your favorite.

YOU WILL NEED:

lightweight paper bag, at least 14 inches wide and 20 inches long, for the cover and the keel
two ⅛-inch dowels, each 18 inches long, for the spars
⅛-inch dowel, 17 inches long, for the spreader bar
flying line
tail
two plastic streamers, each 5 feet long
cloth tape (such as Mystik cloth tape or duct tape)
cellophane tape or package sealing tape
reinforcement rings (optional)
white glue
two 1⅜-inch pin-on drapery hooks

drapery hook

scissors, pencil, measuring stick, decorating materials

WHAT TO DO:
* For steps marked with this symbol, see chapter three for detailed how-to instructions.

1. Trim the open end of the bag so the edges are even. Turn the bag so the trimmed end is at the top. Following the measurements in the illustration, draw the shape shown and cut it out. Be sure to cut through both sides of the bag.
2. Open the cover and note the gusset (folded side panel) in

68

the center. Bring the fold edges of the wings together and tape the gusset closed.

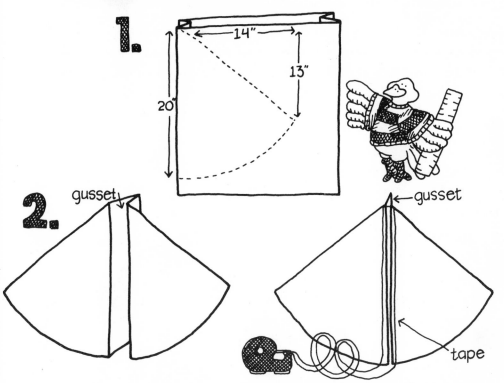

1. 14" · 13" · 20"

2. gusset · gusset · tape

3. To make the keel, cut a rectangle 5 inches wide and 20 inches long from the unused portion of the paper bag or a separate sheet of strong lightweight paper. From one short end, measure over 7 inches and mark a point along the long edge. From this point, draw straight lines to the opposite corners as shown. Cut out the keel along these lines.

3. 20" · 5" · 7"

4. Lay the keel on one side of the gusset, as shown, making sure that the short side of the keel is pointed toward the top of the kite. Glue the keel in place.

5. Trim the gusset so that it is the same shape as the keel. Decorate both the cover and the keel.

* 6. Turn the kite face down. Tape the spars to the wings ½ inch from the leading edges and even with the bottom edge.

7. Using cloth tape, fasten a drapery hook to each end of the spreader bar as shown in the illustration.

* 8. From the top of the kite, measure 11 inches down the side

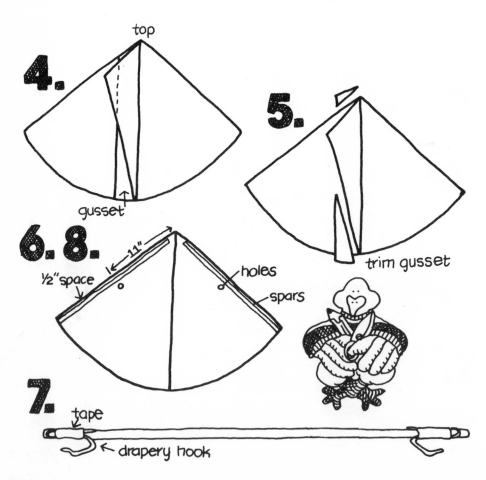

of each wing and poke a small hole beside the inside edges of the spars. Reinforce the holes with tape or cloth rings.

9. Lay the spreader bar across the wings and insert a drapery hook into each hole. The wings should form a slight V-shape when viewed head on.

10. Tape a plastic streamer to the lower tip of each spar and a tail to the base of the gusset.

* 11. Reinforce the edges of the keel with tape, covering the double edges of the gusset at the same time. Poke a hole in the tip of the keel about ½ inch in from the edge as shown. Reinforce the hole and attach the flying line.

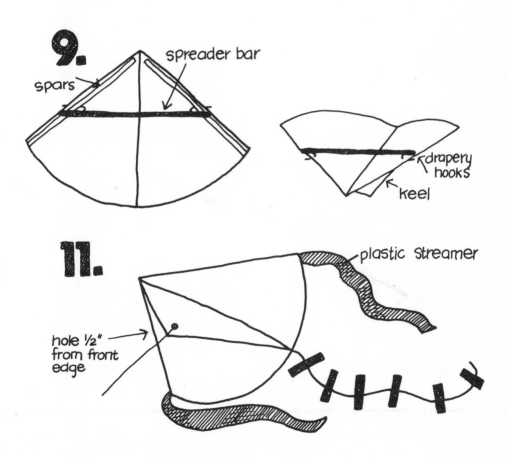

DECORATING TIPS: Color the keel red. For the wings, paint white stars against a dark blue background. While the paint is still wet, dust the stars with gold or silver glitter.

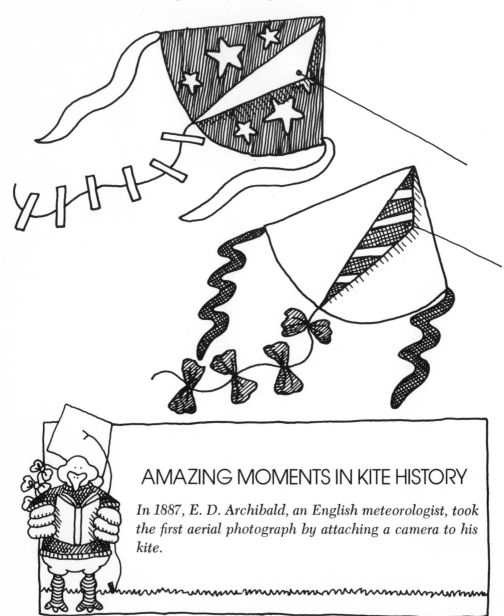

AMAZING MOMENTS IN KITE HISTORY

In 1887, E. D. Archibald, an English meteorologist, took the first aerial photograph by attaching a camera to his kite.

ASTRO GLIDER

The Astro Glider is a high-spirited daredevil of a kite. It climbs swiftly, then swoops and dives as it rides the wind. This exciting kite flies best in moderate winds, but can be flown in lighter winds as well.

YOU WILL NEED:

lightweight paper bag, at least 28 inches long, for the cover and
  the keel
⅛-inch dowel, 22 inches long, for the spar
flying line
tail
cellophane tape or package sealing tape
reinforcement rings (optional)
white glue
scissors, pencil, measuring stick, decorating materials

WHAT TO DO:
* For steps marked with this symbol, see chapter three for detailed how-to instructions.

1. Trim the open end of the bag to make the edges even. Turn the bag so the trimmed end is at the top. Following the

measurements in the illustration, draw the shape shown and cut it out, cutting through both sides of the bag at the same time.

1.

28" ←11"→ 10"

2. Open the cover and note the gusset (folded side panel) in the center. Bring the fold edges of the wings together and tape the gusset closed.

3. To make the keel, cut a rectangle 5 inches wide and 28 inches long from the unused portion of the bag or a separate sheet of strong lightweight paper. From either short side, measure over 7 inches and mark a point along the long edge. From this point, draw straight lines to the opposite corners as shown. Cut out the keel along these lines.

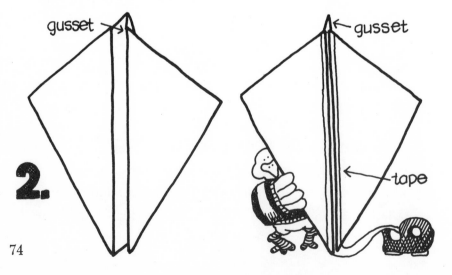

2.

gusset   gusset

tape

3.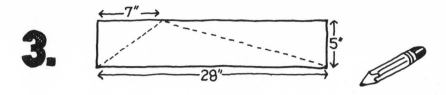

4. Lay the keel on one side of the gusset as shown, making sure that the short side of the keel is pointed toward the top of the kite. Glue the keel in place.

5. Trim the gusset so it is the same shape as the keel. Decorate both the cover and the keel.

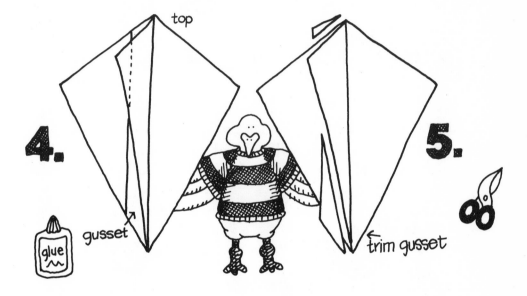

* 6. Turn the kite face down. Tape the spar between the tips of the wings.

7. Tape a tail to the bottom of the kite.

* 8. Reinforce the edges of the keel with tape, covering the double edges of the gusset at the same time. Poke a hole in the tip of the keel about ½ inch in from the edge, as shown, and reinforce. Attach the flying line.

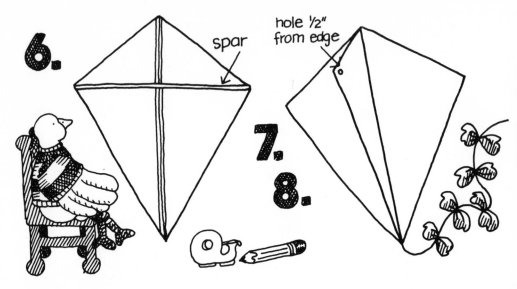

DECORATING TIPS: For a patriotic kite design, draw a line between the tips of the wings, separating the kite into two sections. Decorate the lower sections with red and white stripes. Paint the top part blue with white stars. Make a Firecracker tail, using red, white, and blue paper strips.

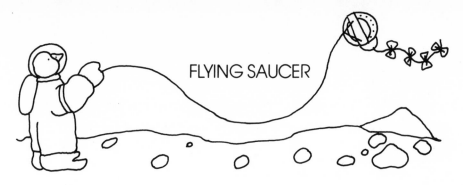

FLYING SAUCER

Don't be surprised if you see some of these alien visitors invading the spring skies. They are top-notch fliers, providing, of course, that a friendly wind is blowing.

YOU WILL NEED:

lightweight paper bag, at least 20 inches long, for the cover
⅛-inch dowel, 19 inches long, for the spine
three ⅛-inch dowels for the spars, two 17 inches long and one 20 inches long
flying line
3-foot bridle cord and towing ring
paper ribbon, 27 inches long
Butterfly tail (see chapter three), using string instead of ribbon for the base
cellophane tape or package sealing tape
reinforcement rings (optional)
pencil and string, at least 14 inches long, for a drawing compass
scissors, measuring stick, decorating materials

WHAT TO DO:
* For steps marked with this symbol, see chapter three for detailed how-to instructions.

1. Knot one end of the string around the lower half of the pencil. Holding the other end of the string at the side edge of the paper bag, draw a half circle with a radius of 10 inches.

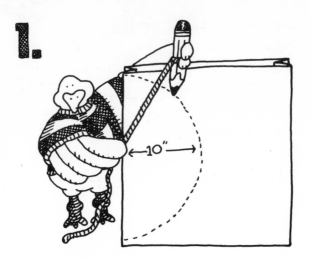

1.

←10"→

2. Cut out the half circle, cutting through both layers of the bag. Open and note the gusset (folded side panel) between the wings.

* 3. Tape the spine to the center of the gusset.

4. Bring the creased edges of the wings together and tape the gusset closed. Turn the kite over. Decorate both the gusset and the wings.

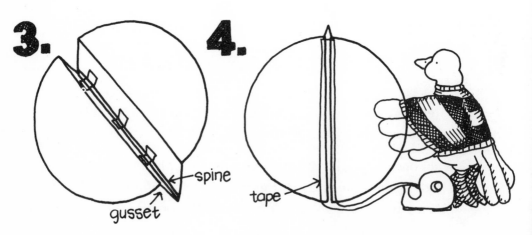

3.

spine

gusset

4.

tape

* 5. Turn the cover face down. Tape the 20-inch spar across the center of the wings as shown.
* 6. Tape the shorter spars parallel to the gusset and 4½ inches from the ends of the crosswise spar.
7. Tape a loop of ribbon to the tips of the shorter spars at either end. Tie on a Butterfly tail to the center of this loop.

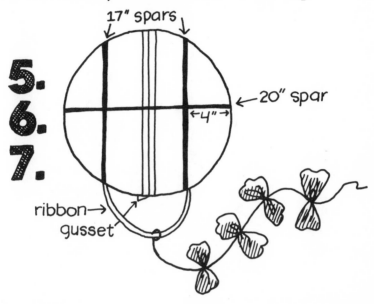

5.
6.
7.

17" spars

←20" spar

←4"→

ribbon→
gusset

AMAZING MOMENTS IN KITE HISTORY

During the Civil War, the Union Army used kites to drop propaganda leaflets behind enemy lines. The leaflets urged the Confederate troops to surrender.

* 8. Poke holes along the inside edge of the spine 2 inches from the top and bottom of the gusset. Reinforce, then tie on the bridle cord as shown.
* 9. Attach the towing ring. Pin or tie on the flying line.

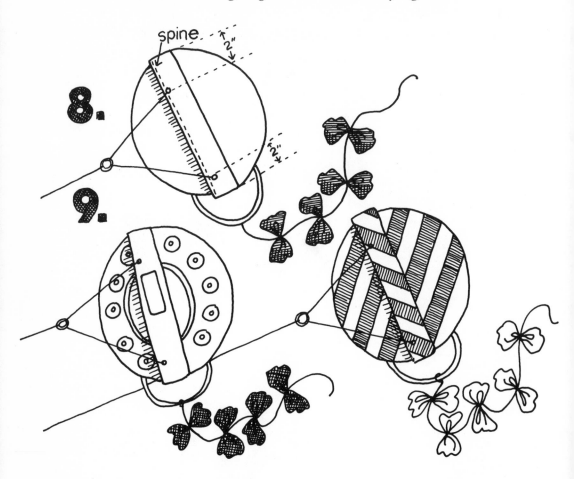

DECORATING TIPS: Don't be tempted to paint your flying saucer silver or gray because it will "vanish" (as all good flying saucers do) once it is airborne. Try a pale yellow paint instead, using blue and black for the details. While the paint is still wet, sprinkle with gold glitter to give it a shiny look.

Sky Monsters

SPACE DEMON

If you look closely, this toothy creature is really a Delta kite in disguise. The sharp "teeth" and long wiggly "legs" are actually tail streamers that help to stabilize the kite in strong winds. This kite is great fun to fly and is guaranteed to attract a crowd of on-lookers wherever it appears.

YOU WILL NEED:

lightweight paper bag, at least 19 inches wide, for the cover and the keel
two ⅛-inch dowels, each 19 inches long, for the spars
⅛-inch dowel, 21 inches long, for the spreader bar
flying line
white plastic trash bag
black plastic trash bag, at least 3 feet long
cloth tape (such as Mystik cloth tape or duct tape)
cellophane tape or package sealing tape
reinforcement rings (optional)
white glue
two 1⅜-inch pin-on drapery hooks
scissors, pencil, measuring stick, decorating materials

81

WHAT TO DO:

* For steps marked with this symbol, see chapter three for detailed how-to instructions.

1. To make the cover, frame, and keel, follow the directions for the Delta kite, steps 1-12, pages 62-65.

2. For the monster's teeth, cut eight triangular strips 4 inches wide and 12 inches long from the white plastic bag. Tape the strips across the bottom of the kite, as shown, leaving 3 inches on each side for the monster's legs.

3. To make the legs, cut two strips 3 inches wide and 6 feet long from the black plastic bag. Tape one strip to each side of the kite at the bottom. Trim the ends to look like claws.

* 4. Reinforce the edges of the keel with tape, covering the double edges of the gusset at the same time. Poke a hole in the tip of the keel about ½ inch in from the edge, as shown, and reinforce. Attach the flying line.

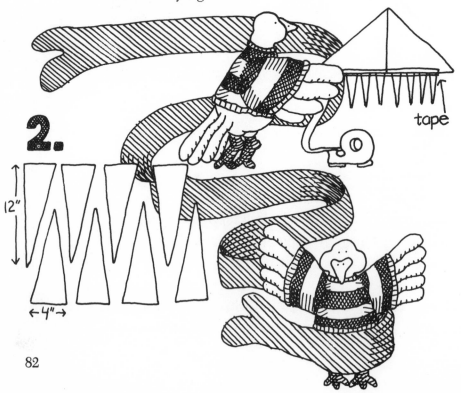

DECORATING TIPS: Paint the wings black and let dry. For the eyes, cut white circles from lightweight paper and glue them in place. Color the centers green. Paint the keel red or any other bright color.

AMAZING MOMENTS IN KITE HISTORY

On April 4, 1976, Kazuhiko Asaba of Kamakura, Japan, flew 1,050 kites on a single flying line . . . a world's record!

CATERPILLAR

This charming kite takes easily to the sky and, once aloft, it is a strong, stable flier. Because of its long swishing tail, it performs best in moderate winds.

YOU WILL NEED:

sheet of strong lightweight paper, 23 inches wide and 18 inches long, for the cover. Do not use newspaper. It tends to bow along the top edge, causing the kite to dive.
⅛-inch dowel, 18 inches long, for the spine
two ⅛-inch dowels for the spars, one 23 inches long and one 13 inches long
two ⅛-inch dowels, each 12 inches long, for reinforcing the tail flying line
3-foot bridle cord and towing ring
large plastic trash bag, at least 2½ feet long
cellophane tape or package sealing tape
reinforcement rings (optional)
scissors, pencil, measuring stick, decorating materials

WHAT TO DO:
* For steps marked with this symbol, see chapter three for detailed how-to instructions.

1. Fold the cover paper in half, bringing the short sides together. Turn the paper so that the fold is at your left.
2. On the side opposite the fold, mark a point 5 inches down from the top. Mark a second point along the bottom edge 6 inches from the fold.

3. Draw the shape shown and cut it out, cutting through both layers of paper at the same time.

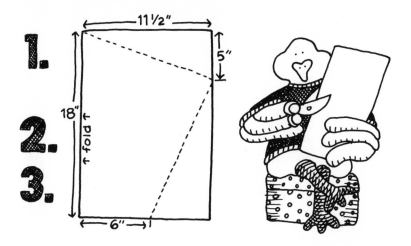

4. Open the cover and lay it flat so the triangular end points upward. Decorate.

* 5. Turn the cover face down. Tape the spine to the center fold.

* 6. Tape the 23-inch spar at the widest point between the tips of the wings. Tape the 13-inch spar across the spine 1 inch from the bottom edge of the cover.

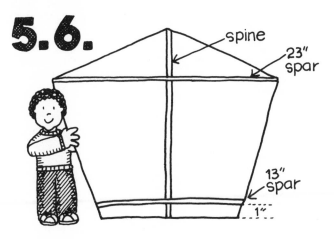

7. From the plastic bag, cut a strip 12 inches wide and 5 feet long. Tape one end to the base of the kite. Run tape along both sides and press firmly.

8. Tape one of the reinforcing dowels to the plastic strip 14 inches below the base of the kite. Tape the second dowel 14 inches below the first.

9. From the unused portion of the plastic bag, make a Strip or Butterfly tail (see chapter three) and tape it to the bottom edge of the plastic strip. Start with a tail about 10 feet long.

* 10. Poke holes for the bridle cord 1 inch from the top and bottom of the spine. Reinforce.

* 11. Turn the kite face up. Attach the bridle cord and the towing ring. Pin or tie on the flying line.

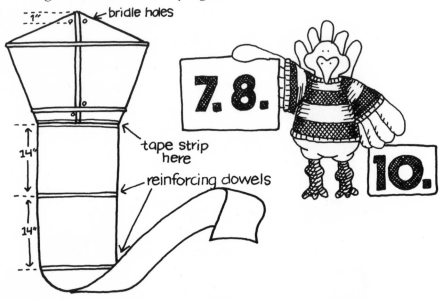

DECORATING TIPS: Paint the caterpillar's face with any bright colors. (How about a yellow or pink caterpillar with an orange nose?) Outline the features with heavy black lines. Glue on strips of shiny gift wrapping for antennae. Add paper tassels (see chapter three) if you like.

SNOWBIRD

Here is a kite to send your spirits soaring. As it sails aloft, the tail streamers flutter softly, giving the uncanny illusion of a bird in flight. Lightweight, yet surprisingly strong, the Snowbird flies well in both light and moderate winds. If the spreader bar is removed, the kite collapses and may be rolled up for easy storage.

YOU WILL NEED:

white plastic trash bag, at least 21 inches wide and 29½ inches long, for the cover and the keel

two ⅛-inch dowels, each 17 inches long, for the spars

⅛-inch dowel, 29½ inches long, for the spine

⅛-inch dowel, 17½ inches long, for the spreader bar

flying line

plastic streamer, 5 to 10 feet long depending on the wind (see chapter three)

two 1⅜-inch pin-on drapery hooks

cloth tape (such as Mystik cloth tape or duct tape)

cellophane tape or package sealing tape

reinforcement rings (optional)

felt-tip pen or crayon for marking on plastic, scissors, measuring stick, decorating materials

WHAT TO DO:

* For steps marked with this symbol, see chapter three for detailed how-to instructions.

    1. From the plastic bag, cut a sheet 21 inches square.

* 2. Tape the spine between two opposite corners.

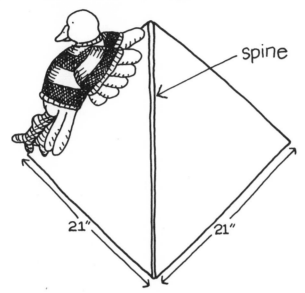

    3. To make the keel, cut a rectangle 5 inches wide and 29½ inches long from the unused portion of the plastic bag. Measure over 8 inches from either short side and mark a point along the long edge. From this point, draw lines to the opposite corners of the rectangle. Cut out the keel along these lines.

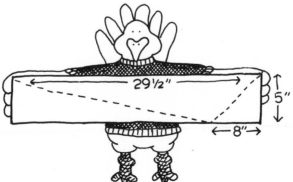

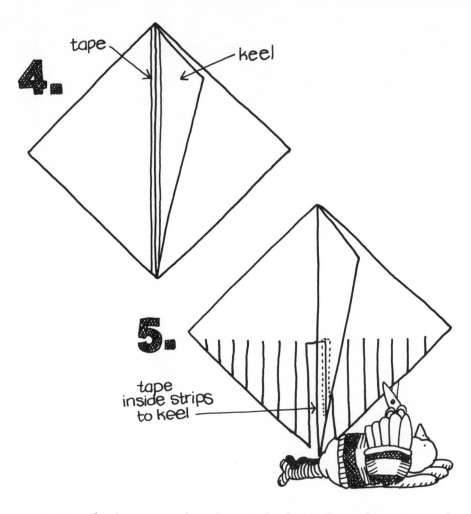

4. Lay the long straight edge of the keel along the spine and tape it in place. Run tape on both sides of the keel and press firmly.

5. Turn the kite so that the short side of the keel is at the top. Starting at the lower edge of the cover, cut slits 1½ inches apart to the center of the wings. Leave a ½-inch strip on each side of the spine. Fold these strips onto the keel and secure with tape.

6. Decorate the cover and the keel.

* 7. Turn the kite face down. Tape the spars to the uncut sides of the wings ½ inch from the edges as shown.

  8. Using cloth tape, fasten a drapery hook to each end of the spreader bar as shown in the illustration.

* 9. On the inside edge of each spar, mark a point 11½ inches from the top of the kite. Poke a small hole at these points and reinforce with tape or cloth rings.

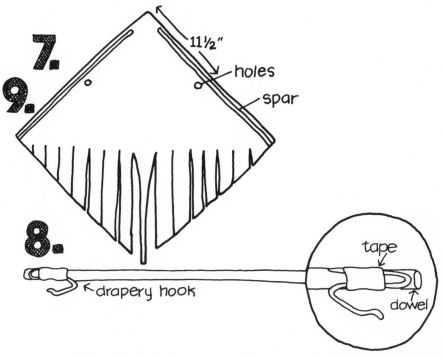

10. Place the spreader bar across the wings and insert a drapery hook into each hole. The wings should form a slight V-shape when viewed head on.

11. Attach a 5-foot streamer to the base of the spine. Double the length of the streamer in stronger winds.

* 12. Poke a hole in the tip of the keel about ½ inch from the edge as shown. Reinforce the opening with tape or cloth rings on each side of the keel. Attach the flying line.

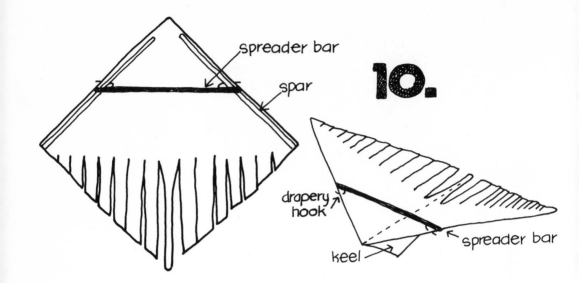

spreader bar

spar

10.

drapery hook

spreader bar

keel

DECORATING TIPS: Draw the bird's face and feather markings with a crayon or felt marker. Any colors will do as long as they can be seen easily from a distance. Be sure to draw the beak and eye on each side of the keel.

FLYING DRAGON

The Flying Dragon is one of the many beautiful and unusual kites that is native to Thailand. Over eighteen feet long, this fiery monster creates a dazzling spectacle as it soars across the sky. Despite its size, the Dragon kite is easy to fly but needs a good steady wind to send it aloft.

YOU WILL NEED:

sheet of strong lightweight paper, 20 inches wide and 16 inches long, for the cover
⅛-inch dowel, 16 inches long, for the spine
two ⅛-inch dowels for the spars, one 20 inches long and one 14¼ inches long
two ⅛-inch dowels, each 4 inches long, for reinforcing the cover
flying line
3-foot bridle cord and towing ring
two large plastic trash bags, at least 28 inches wide and 36 inches long
cellophane tape or package sealing tape
scissors, pencil, measuring stick, decorating materials

AMAZING MOMENTS IN KITE HISTORY

During World War II, kites bearing pictures of enemy aircraft were used by the United States Navy for target practice.

WHAT TO DO:

* For steps marked with this symbol, see chapter three for detailed how-to instructions.

1. Fold the cover paper in half, bringing the short sides together. Turn the paper so that the fold is at your left.
2. On the side opposite the fold, mark a point 5½ inches from the top. Mark a second point along the bottom edge 7 inches from the fold.
3. Draw the shape shown and cut it out, cutting through both layers of paper at the same time.
4. Open the cover and lay it flat with the curved edge at the top. Decorate.

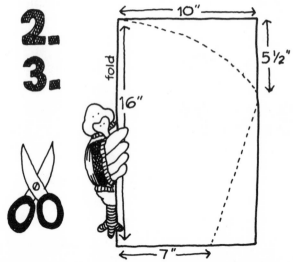

* 5. Turn the cover face down. Tape the spine to the center fold.
* 6. Tape the 20-inch spar between the tips of the wings at their widest point. Tape the shorter spar 1 inch from the bottom edge of the cover.
7. Lay the reinforcing dowels midway between the top of the spine and the tips of the wings as shown. Secure with tape in the same way as for the spars.

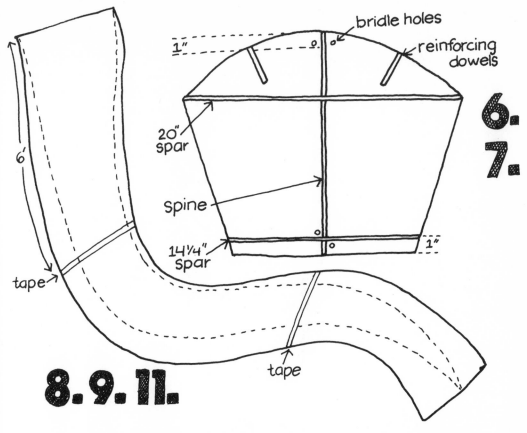

bridle holes

reinforcing dowels

1"

20" spar

spine

14¼" spar

6'

tape

1"

6.
7.

8. 9. 11.

tape

8. For the tail cut three strips, each 14 inches wide and 6 feet long, from the plastic bags. Tape the strips together end to end.

9. Cut down the sides of the tail so they gradually taper to a point. (This is easier to do if you fold the tail in half lengthwise and cut both sides at the same time.)

10. Tape the straight end of the tail to the bottom of the kite. Run tape along both sides and press firmly.

* 11. Poke holes for the bridle cord 1 inch from the top and bottom of the spine and reinforce.

* 12. Turn the kite face up. Attach the bridle cord and the towing ring. Pin or tie on the flying line.

DECORATING TIPS: Use bold colors for the dragon's face such as yellow, green, and red. Outline the features with black. Paint yellow scales along the tail.

OCTOPUS

The Octopus kite is a variation of the Flying Dragon. It is a spectacular kite that is almost as much fun to make as it is to fly. Like its paper cousin, the Octopus should be flown in a steady breeze.

YOU WILL NEED:

sheet of strong lightweight paper, 20 inches wide and 16 inches long, for the cover
⅛-inch dowel, 16 inches long, for the spine
two ⅛-inch dowels for the spars, one 20 inches long and one 14¼ inches long
two ⅛-inch dowels, each 4 inches long, for reinforcing the cover
flying line
3-foot bridle cord and towing ring
large black or green plastic trash bag
cellophane tape or package sealing tape
reinforcement rings (optional)
scissors, pencil, measuring stick

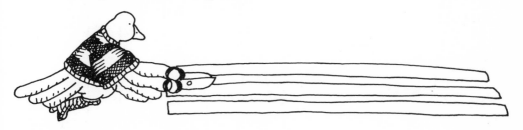

WHAT TO DO:
* For steps marked with this symbol, see chapter three for detailed how-to instructions.

1. To make the cover, follow the directions for the Flying Dragon kite, steps 1-7, pages 94-95.

2. Cut the plastic bag into strips 2½ inches wide. Tape the strips together to form five streamers about 10 feet long. Tape the ends of the streamers evenly across the bottom of the cover.

* 3. Poke holes for the bridle cord 1 inch from the top and bottom of the spine and reinforce.

* 4. Turn the kite face up. Attach the bridle cord and the towing ring. Pin or tie on the flying line.

DECORATING TIPS: Color the cover to match the tail streamers. For the eyes, cut ovals from thin white paper and glue them in place. Paint the centers purple or pink.

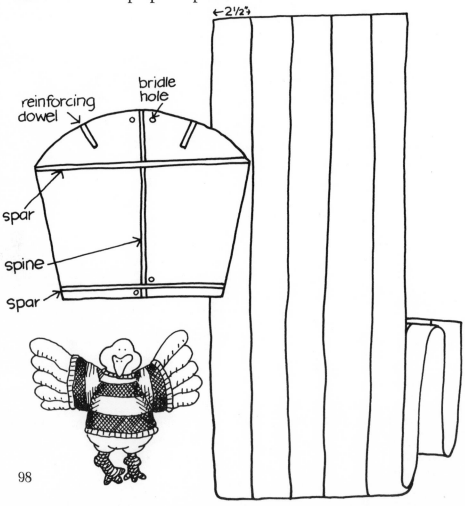

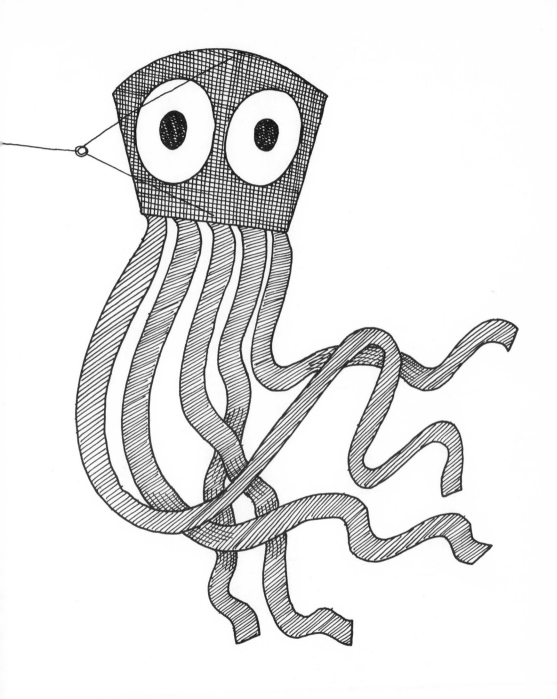

FLYING YOUR KITE

Now that you've built a kite, it's time to send it soaring up into the clouds. But before you head for the nearest flying field, there are some important things you'll need to discover. Like any good pilot, you'll want to know the most favorable weather conditions for your aircraft, the best and safest flying techniques, where to find a good launching site, and what problems you might face and how to cope with them. Your kite-flying will also be smoother if you understand some principles of aerodynamics—why and how a kite flies. All of these things are essential to the making of a successful flight.

THE SECRET OF FLIGHT

A kite is heavier than air, so why does it fly? Why does it defy gravity and soar upward instead of falling to the ground like a leaf? The answers to these questions involve some basic scientific principles. Knowing and understanding these principles will help you to become a more skillful and proficient flier.

An airplane, like a kite, defies the law of gravity, but an airplane has an engine to thrust it forward. A kite must rely solely on the wind to support it. Without wind, a kite will simply not fly.

There are three forces that act upon the kite to keep it aloft—*lift, gravity,* and *drag.* Lift is the upward force supplied by the wind. Gravity, as you know, is a force that tends to pull the kite downward. Drag is the resistance of the air to the movement of the kite. Kite tails produce extra drag and are used to balance the lifting force of the wind. In high winds, a longer tail is needed because the force of lift is so much greater.

When the forces of gravity and drag equal the force of lift, a kite tends to float in one place. But when the forces of gravity and drag are greater, it will drift or dive to the ground.

One of the basic reasons that a kite rises is because its face is tipped forward into the wind. As the wind pushes against the kite, it forces the kite backward and upward. At the same time, the flying line pulls downward, holding the kite steady so that it can maintain its angle of flight.

If for some reason a kite should move into another position so that it can no longer catch the wind, it will fall. For example, if a kite flies directly overhead (which can happen if it is allowed to climb too quickly), it may flatten out and fly parallel to the ground. Since the wind can no longer push against the cover, the kite will either loop or go into a dive. Changes in the wind can also cause a kite to lose its angle of flight. The wind can shift suddenly or simply stop blowing. Sometimes a strong gust can drive a kite to the ground.

CHOOSING YOUR LAUNCH PAD

Parks, playgrounds, and open fields are good places for flying kites. A beach is an ideal place if it is not too crowded. You will need plenty of room to move around once your kite is in the air.

Look for large open areas away from buildings and trees that might block the wind and get in your way. Most important, stay clear of overhead wires. They are dangerous and should always be avoided.

For safety, don't fly a kite near an airport or a public highway. Sometimes kites can cause accidents, so be wise and careful about your flying site selection.

WIND CONDITIONS

Most people believe that spring is the best time of year for flying kites. But for many lightweight kites, the gentle breezes of summer and early fall are better than strong gusty March winds. Kite-flying really has no season. If you live where the winters are mild, you can fly all year round as long as the wind is blowing and the weather is clear.

The kites in this book will fly best in steady winds between four and twelve miles per hour. However, even within this range there are individual differences in ideal wind speeds. The following chart will help you to estimate wind speeds and to determine the best flying conditions for each of your kites. If you can, it is a good idea to take two or three kites from different wind speed categories to the flying field. Then you will be prepared for a variety of wind conditions, changes which may occur quite rapidly.

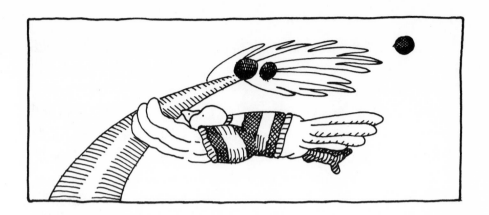

WIND SPEED/ MILES PER HOUR	WINDS	WIND EFFECTS	SPECIAL INSTRUCTIONS
1-3	Calm	Leaves not moving. Smoke drifting lazily.	Not quite enough wind for flying.
4-7	Light	Leaves rustling. Wind can be felt on face.	Good winds for light-weight kites such as the Two-stick, Snow-bird, and Plastic Diamond.
8-12	Moderate	Leaves and twigs in constant motion. Small flags waving.	Ideal winds for all but lightest kites. Keep eyes on the treetops. If branches start to sway, fly with caution.
13 and upward	Strong	Treetops tossing, dust flying, papers blowing.	Winds are too gusty for paper and plastic kites.

(This table has been adapted from the Beaufort scale of wind force used by the U.S. Weather Bureau.)

Check your kite over carefully before you fly it. Adjust the towing ring if necessary. Make sure the spars are firmly in place and all knots are tied securely.

If the wind is steady, it is easy to launch the kite by yourself. This is how to do it. Stand with your back to the wind and hold the kite up high by its bridle or keel. When you feel a firm breeze, gently cast the kite into the air and let the wind carry it aloft. As the kite rises, feed the line out evenly, keeping it stretched as tightly as possible.

Once it is airborne, continue to keep the line taut. If the kite drifts downward, quickly reel in the line until it is tight again. Then hold the reel steady without unwinding and watch the kite soar upward.

wind direction

wind direction

If it goes into a power dive, rapidly let out extra line. The sagging line will help to balance the kite until it rights itself. Sometimes it helps to run toward the falling kite, letting out line as you go.

Tug firmly if you want the kite to climb. When it tugs back, release the line slowly—a little at a time.

When the wind is light and unsteady, get a friend to help with the launching. Your friend can hold the kite while you pull on the line. Stand about twenty-five feet apart. When a good wind comes along, signal your friend to "let go." At the same time, walk backward *into* the wind. Tug sharply on the line until the kite begins to rise. Then let the line out slowly.

On calm days when there is little wind, don't try to launch a kite by running with it. Running may get a kite into the air, but chances are it won't stay there very long.

TIP: It is a good idea to take a small repair kit with you whenever you go flying. It should include a pair of scissors, some string, tape, dowels, and extra tail material. Carry these supplies in a cloth or paper shopping bag. Your kit will come in handy if you have to replace a spar, fix a torn cover, extend a tail, or make any number of on-the-spot repairs.

WHAT TO DO IF . . .

IF YOUR KITE WOBBLES AND REFUSES TO CLIMB—Try moving the towing ring a little closer to the top of the bridle cord. (See page 33.) You may have to adjust it two or three times until it is just right.

IF YOUR KITE CLIMBS BUT NOT VERY HIGH—The tail might be too long. Cut off a little, about an arm's length, then launch the kite again.

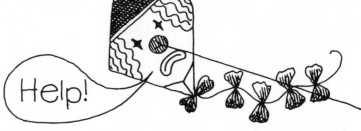

IF YOUR KITE DARTS AND ZIGZAGS—Usually this means it needs a longer tail. Tie on an extra yard or two, then add more if necessary. You should always carry extra tail material with you for just such an emergency.

If your kite is still unsteady, the wind might be too strong for it. Bring the kite down slowly to avoid breaking the spars.

IF YOUR KITE LEANS TO ONE SIDE AND DIVES UPON TAKEOFF—It may not be properly balanced. Make sure that all spars, tassels, and streamers are the same weight and size and placed in the same relative position on each of the wings.

IF YOUR KITE WON'T FLY AT ALL—There may be something wrong with the way it is constructed. Read the instructions again to make sure you followed each step correctly. *Recheck all measurements.* Perhaps the cover paper is too heavy or the decoration has weighted it down. It is always possible that the wind is just not strong enough for the kite you are flying. Try launching it on a windier day.

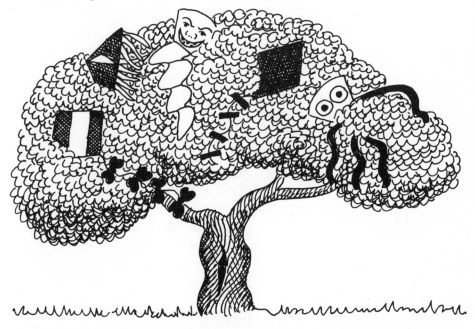

IF YOUR KITE BECOMES SNAGGED IN A TREETOP—Don't climb the tree to rescue it. It's not worth risking an injury to save a kite. If you're patient, a sudden gust of wind might free the kite for you. Sometimes "walking" the line or gentle tuggings will pry it loose. If not, leave the kite in the tree. You can always make another one.

IF YOUR KITE FALLS—Don't drag it across the ground. Walk over to it, winding the line as you go. Check the kite for broken spars or rips in the cover. Make any necessary repairs before launching it again.

IF YOUR FLYING LINE BECOMES BADLY TANGLED—Cut out the snarled part. Then knot the ends back together as shown in the illustration. This is a strong knot that won't come loose. With practice, you will be able to tie it easily.

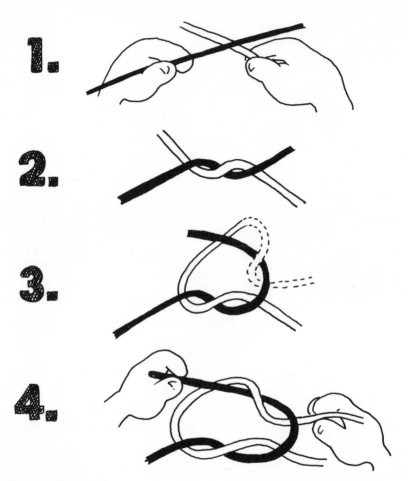

PAPER CLIMBERS

When your kite is flying smoothly, it's fun to send paper climbers up the flying line. To make a climber, cut a circle or square from construction paper. Poke a hole in the center. Then cut a slit from the outside edge to the hole.

Slip the paper onto the flying line and tape the slit closed. With luck, the wind will catch the paper and carry it aloft.

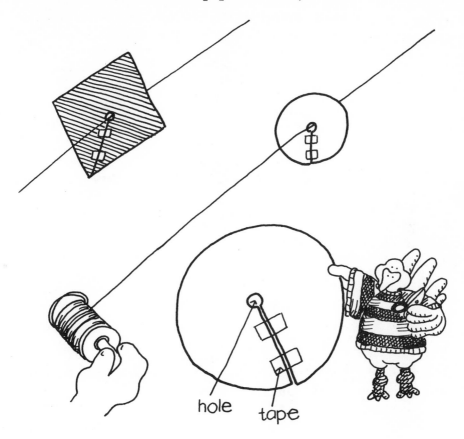

hole   tape

HAPPY LANDINGS

When you're ready to bring the kite down, there is one important rule to remember: *Take your time*. Reel the line in slowly and evenly no matter how long it takes.

In stronger winds when the kite is pulling hard, it is best to walk toward the kite as you reel it in. This helps to relieve the tension on the line. When the kite is nearly down, let the line go slack. This will prevent a last-minute crashing dive. With luck, the kite will flutter softly to the ground.

If the kite loops and dives as you reel it in, it may be necessary to "walk" it down. This is easy to do but you'll need a friend to help. Have your friend operate the reel. Then slide the line under your arm and walk slowly toward the kite. Walk a few steps at a time until you and the kite are face-to-face.

KITE SAFETY

Expert or beginner, all kite fliers should observe these few simple rules:

- Never fly a kite in the rain or if a storm is approaching. You could get severely shocked from electricity that builds up in the clouds.
- Never use wire for a flying line.
- If your kite gets entangled in an overhead wire, *leave it there!*

Don't yank wildly on the flying line or throw things at the kite to free it.

- When your kite pulls hard, the flying line can slip through your fingers and cut them. To protect your hands, wear a pair of lightweight leather or cotton gloves.
- On bright days, try to wear a brimmed hat and dark glasses. They will protect your eyes if your kite flies "into" the sun.
- Never fly a kite in the street or near a busy roadway. Play it safe. Use good common sense when choosing a place to fly.

KITE TOURNAMENTS

Every year, from spring until late fall, kite tournaments are held in cities and towns across the country. These colorful events give kite fliers a chance to get together, compete, and exchange ideas. Check your local newspaper, radio and TV stations, and community bulletin boards for announcements of competitions to be held in your area.

If you have an opportunity to compete, it is a good idea to take a friend along to help with the launching. Practice with your helper beforehand so he or she will know exactly what to do. Plan on taking at least two kites—one for light and one for moderate winds. And don't forget your repair kit in case of a mishap.

Rules vary from one contest to another. Just be sure that you know and understand the rules before the tournament begins. Categories of competition vary also, but usually awards are given for the most beautiful kite, the most original design, the largest and smallest kites, and the highest flier.

But win or lose, it's all in fun. And everyone—spectators and contestants alike—has a good time.

LIST OF SUPPLY SOURCES

Not too many years ago, kites could only be purchased in drug-stores, toy stores, five-and-tens, and the like. But today there are shops that sell nothing but kites—all shapes, colors, and sizes—plus kite books, kite-making supplies, and accessories. The number of these colorful shops is still relatively small, but it is getting larger every year.

The following stores in the United States and Canada sell kites and related items. Since not all states are represented, we've also indicated those shops that accept mail order and/or have catalogs available at little or no cost. Write or call these stores for details concerning their specific ordering requirements. For new shops that may have opened since this list was compiled, check the Yellow Pages of your phone book under "Kites."

ALASKA

Whittlewinds Gallery
600 E. Northern Lights
Anchorage 99503
(907) 278-9434
Stocks: kites, kite accessories, kite-
    making supplies, kite books
Open: year round

CALIFORNIA

Come Fly A Kite
P.O. Box 132
Carmel 93921
(408) 624-3422
Stocks: kites, kite books; specializes
    in cloth kites
Open: year round
Mail order and catalog available

The Red Balloon
In the Vineyard
1517-15 East Valley Parkway
Escondido 92027
(714) 741-5011
Stocks: kites, kite books
Open: year round

Let's Fly A Kite
Fisherman's Village
13763 Fiji Way
Marina del Rey 90291
(213) 822-2561
Stocks: kites, kite accessories, kite-
making supplies, kite books
Open: year round

Kites Are Up
2209 West Balboa Boulevard
Newport Beach 92663
(714) 675-2473
Stocks: kites, kite accessories, kite-
making supplies, kite books
Open: year round

Kites Kites Kites
Jack London Village
55 Alice Street
Oakland 94607
(415) 444-0550
Stocks: kites, kite accessories, kite
books
Open: year round

The Kite Store
973 Grand Avenue
Pacific Beach 92109
(714) 270-2692
Stocks: kites, kite accessories, kite-
making supplies, kite books
Open: year round

Sunshine Kite Company
233-B Fisherman's Wharf
Redondo Beach Pier
Redondo Beach 90277
(213) 372-0308
Stocks: kites, kite accessories, kite-
making supplies, kite books;
specializes in fighter kites
Open: year round
Mail order and catalog available

Kites & Strings
740 Ventura Place
San Diego 92109
(714) 488-KITE
Stocks: kites, kite accessories, kite-
making supplies, kite books;
specializes in air-brush cloth,
diamond kites
Open: year round
Mail order

Come Fly A Kite, Inc.
Ghiradelli Square
900 North Point
San Francisco 94109
(415) 441-2965
Stocks: kites, kite accessories, kite-
making supplies, kite books;
specializes in white bird cloth kites
Open: year round
Mail order and catalog available

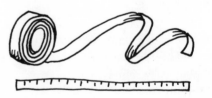

High As A Kite
761 Beach
San Francisco 94901
Stocks: kites, kite accessories, kite-
making supplies, kite books
Open: year round
Mail order and catalog available

Kite & Gift, Inc.
Fisherman's Wharf
333 Jefferson Street, No. 7
San Francisco 94133
(415) 885-5785
Stocks: kites, kite accessories, kite-
making supplies, kite books
Open: year round
Mail order

Krazy Kites
1745 Nipomo Street
San Luis Obispo 93401
(805) 541-3127
Stocks: kites, kite accessories, kite-
making supplies, kite books;
specializes in cloth and spools
Open: year round
Mail order

Fly A Kite
South Coast Village
3850 South Plaza Drive
Santa Ana 92704
(714) 545-2849
Stocks: kites, kite accessories, kite-
making supplies, kite books
Open: year round
Mail order

You've Got Me Flying Kite Shop
123 Pearl Alley
Santa Cruz 95060
(408) 426-4444
Stocks: kites, kite accessories, kite-
making supplies, kite books
Open: year round

High As A Kite
691 Bridgeway
Sausalito 94965
(415) 332-8944
Stocks, kites, kite accessories, kite-
making supplies, kite books
Open: year round
Mail order and catalog available

Fly A Kite
19800 Hawthorne Boulevard
Torrance 90503
(213) 371-4442
Stocks: kites, kite accessories, kite-
making supplies, kite books
Open: year round
Mail order

COLORADO

Sunshine Kites
308 South Hunter Street
Aspen 81611
(303) 925-4540
Stocks: kites and accessories, kite
  books
Open: year round
Mail order and catalog available

The Kite Store in Larimer Square
1415 Larimer Square
Denver 80202
(303) 623-2353
Stocks: kites, kite accessories, kite-
  making supplies, kite books
Open: year round
Mail order

Sky Scrapers Kites
2563 Fifteenth Street
Denver 80211
(303) 433-9518
Stocks: kites, kite accessories, kite-
  making supplies, kite books
Open: year round
Mail order and catalog available

CONNECTICUT

The Ben Franklin Kite Shoppe
One-Half Pearl Street
Mystic 06355
(203) 536-0220
Stocks: kites, kite accessories, kite-
  making supplies, kite books;
  specializes in books, building
  supplies, braided nylon
Open: year round
Mail order and catalog available

DISTRICT OF COLUMBIA

The Kite Site
3101 M Street, N.W.
Georgetown 20007
(202) 965-4230
Stocks: kites, kite accessories, kite-
  making supplies, kite books
Open: year round
Mail order and catalog available

FLORIDA

Come Fly A Kite
313 Clearwater Mall
International Bazaar, 2nd Level
Clearwater 33518
(813) 796-1613
Stocks: kites, kite accessories, kite-
  making supplies, kite books
Open: year round

Heavenly Body Kites
409 Greene Street
Key West 33040
(305) 296-2535
Stocks: kites, kite accessories, kite-
making supplies, kite books
Open: year round
Mail order and catalog available

HAWAII

High As A Kite
International Marketplace
Kalakaua Avenue
Honolulu 96815
(808) 923-3446
Stocks: kites, kite accessories, kite
books
Open: year round
Mail order and catalog available

High As A Kite
Kona Village
Alii Drive
Kailua-Kona 96740
(808) 329-5566
same as Honolulu store

Starships & Strings
75-5699-D Alii Drive
Kailua-Kona 96740
(808) 329-5330
Stocks: kites, kite accessories, kite-
making supplies
Open: year round

High As A Kite
Coconut Plantation
484 Kuhu Highway
Kapa Kanai 96740
(808) 822-9083
same as Honolulu store

High As A Kite
703 Front Street
Lahaina, Maui 96761
(808) 661-3159
Stocks: kites, kite accessories, kite-
making supplies, kite books
Open: year round
Mail order and catalog available

KANSAS

Magnificent Wings of the Wind Kite
Gallery
1223 East First
Wichita 67214
(316) 267-2290
Stocks: kites, kite accessories, kite-
making supplies, kite books;
specializes in Hearts Delight kites
Open: year round
Mail order and catalog available

LOUISIANA

The Kite Shop-Jackson Square
542 St. Peter Street
New Orleans 70116
(504) 524-0028
Stocks: kites, kite accessories, kite-
  making supplies, kite books
Open: year round
Mail order and catalog available

MAINE

Say Hi Kites
3 Wharf Street
Portland 04101
(207) 772-0277
Stocks: kites, kite accessories, kite-
  making supplies, kite books
Open: April-December

MARYLAND

Kites Aweigh
36 Market Street
Annapolis 21401
(301) 268-6065
Stocks: kites, kite accessories, kite-
  making supplies, kite books
Open: year round

The Kite Loft
5 North Second Street
Ocean City 21842
(301) 289-6864
Stocks: kites, kite accessories, kite-
  making supplies, kite books
Open: May-September
Mail order

MASSACHUSETTS

Soft As A Grape
36 Boylston Street
Cambridge 02138
(617) 491-1988
Stocks: kites, kite accessories, kite-
  making supplies, kite books
Open: year round

Soft As A Grape
251 Main Street
Falmouth 02540
(617) 548-9871
Stocks: kites, kite books
Open: April-December

Outermost Kites
240 Commercial Street
Provincetown, Cape Cod 02657
(617) 487-3766
Stocks: kites and related items, kite
  books
Open: March-December
Mail order

120

MISSOURI

The Emporium
606 Ship Street
St. Joseph 49085
(616) 983-0404
Stocks: kites and accessories, kite
    books
Open: year round
Mail order and catalog available

NEW YORK

Go Fly A Kite, Inc.
1434 Third Avenue
New York 10028
(212) 988-8885
Stocks: kites, kite accessories, kite
    books
Open: year round
Mail order and catalog available

Go Fly A Kite, Inc.
79 Job's Lane
Southampton (branch of New York
    store)
Open: May-September

NORTH CAROLINA

Kitty Hawk Kites
P.O. Box 386
Bypass 158
Nags Head 27959
(919) 441-7575
Stocks: kites, kite books
Open: year round
Mail order

NORTH DAKOTA

The Kite Farm
Box 338
Medora 58645
(701) 623-4455
Stocks: kites, kite accessories, kite-
    making supplies, kite books
Mail order

OHIO

The Kite Kompany, Inc.
33 West Orange
Chagrin Falls 44022
(216) 247-4223
Stocks: kites, kite accessories, kite-
    making supplies, kite books
Open: March-December
Mail order and catalog available

The Cloud Crowd
19 Bennington Drive
Dayton 45405
(513) 274-9683
Stocks: kites, kite accessories, kite-
    making supplies, kite books
Open: year round
Mail order

OREGON

Kites and Other Delights
99 West 10th Street, Suite 111
Eugene 97401
(503) 345-4856
Stocks: kites, kite accessories, kite-
making supplies, kite books
Open: year round

Wind Play
212 N.W. Couch
Portland 97209
(503) 223-1760
Stocks: kites, kite accessories, kite-
making supplies, kite books;
specializes in easy-to-make and
one-of-a-kind kites
Open: year round
Mail order and catalog available

TENNESSEE

Wonderful Word of Kites
B-1 Mountain Mall
Gatlinburg 37738
(615) 436-6470
Stocks: kites, kite books
Open: year round
Mail order and catalog available

VIRGINIA

Krazy Kites
Virginia Beach Fishing Pier
Virginia Beach 23451
(804) 422-5483
Stocks: kites, kite accessories, kite-
making supplies, kite books
Open: April-October

WASHINGTON

Great Winds Kites
Pioneer Square
166 South Jackson Street
Seattle 98104
(206) 624-6886
Stocks: kites, kite accessories, kite-
making supplies, kite books
Open: year round
Mail order and catalog available

WISCONSIN

Fish Creek Kite Company
R.R. 1   Box 205   Highway 42
Fish Creek 54212
(414) 868-3769
Stocks: kites, kite accessories, kite-
making supplies, kite books
Open: May-October

CANADA

Catch The Wind, Ltd.
329 8 Avenue, Southwest
Calgary, Alberta T2P 1C4
(403) 265-4747
Stocks: kites, kite accessories, kite-
  making supplies, kite books
Open: year round
Mail order and catalog available

Kites On A String
114 Kingway Garden Mall
Edmonton, Alberta T5G 3A6
(403) 471-4018
Stocks: kites, kite accessories, kite-
  making supplies, kite books
Open: year round
Mail order

High As A Kite
201-131 Water Street
Vancouver, B.C. V6B 4M3
(604) 687-8041
Stocks: kites, kite accessories, kite-
  making supplies, kite books
Open: year round
Mail order and catalog available

The Kite Store
848-A Yonge Street
Toronto, Ontario M4W 2H1
(416) 964-0434
Stocks: kites, kite accessories, kite-
  making supplies, kite books
Open: year round
Mail order and catalog available

KITE ORGANIZATIONS AND INFORMATION

The American Kitefliers Association is an international organization devoted to the promotion and advancement of kite-flying. It boasts members in the United States and Canada as well as from twenty-seven other countries. Anyone is eligible to join. The only requirement is an interest in kites. For membership information, write to:

> American Kitefliers Association
> Welca D. Braswell, President
> 10,000 Lomond Drive
> Manassas, Virginia 22110.

There are also numerous kite clubs and associations throughout the United States and the world in addition to local chapters of the American Kitefliers Association. For information about the group nearest you, write to the address above.

KITE LINES

Kite Lines (formerly *Kite Tales*) is a magazine written exclusively for kitefliers. For subscription information, write to:

> *Kite Lines*
> 7106 Campfield Road
> Baltimore, Maryland 21207.

METRIC CONVERSION CHART

The measurements used in this book are given in inches and feet. To convert these figures to the metric system, use the following chart. (Equivalent measurements are approximate.)

⅛ inch	= 3 mm	17 inches	= 43 cm
½ inch	= 1.25 cm	17½ inches	= 44.50 cm
⅝ inch	= 1.50 cm	18 inches	= 45.50 cm
¾ inch	= 2 cm	19 inches	= 48 cm
1 inch	= 2.50 cm	20 inches	= 51 cm
1⅜ inches	= 3.50 cm	21 inches	= 53.50 cm
1½ inches	= 4 cm	21¼ inches	= 54 cm
2 inches	= 5 cm	22 inches	= 56 cm
2½ inches	= 6.50 cm	23 inches	= 58.50 cm
3 inches	= 7.50 cm	24 inches	= 61 cm
3⅔ inches	= 9.50 cm	25 inches	= 63.50 cm
4 inches	= 10 cm	27 inches	= 68.50 cm
4½ inches	= 11.50 cm	28 inches	= 71 cm
5 inches	= 12.50 cm	29 inches	= 73.50 cm
5½ inches	= 14 cm	29½ inches	= 75 cm
6 inches	= 15 cm	30 inches	= 76 cm
7 inches	= 18 cm	32 inches	= 81 cm
8 inches	= 20.50 cm	33 inches	= 84 cm
8½ inches	= 21.50 cm	36 inches	= 91.50 cm
10 inches	= 25.50 cm	40 inches	= 1 m
11 inches	= 28 cm		
11½ inches	= 29 cm	2 feet	= 61 cm
12 inches	= 30.50 cm	2½ feet	= 76 cm
12½ inches	= 31.50 cm	3 feet	= 91.50 cm
13 inches	= 33 cm	5 feet	= 1.50 m
14 inches	= 35.50 cm	10 feet	= 3 m
14¼ inches	= 36 cm	100 feet	= 30 m
15 inches	= 38 cm	300 feet	= 90 m
16 inches	= 40.50 cm		

mm = millimeter   cm = centimeter   m = meter

INDEX

ABOUT THE AUTHORS

Burton and Rita Marks caught kite fever when they introduced their young children to the pleasures of flying homemade kites. Though their sons are now teenage, the Markses are still avid kite aficionados, being members of the American Kite Fliers Association and the Ohio Society for the Elevation of Kites. Burton Marks, a free-lance writer, designer, and artist, and Rita Marks, a teacher, made their children's book debut with Lothrop's *Give a Magic Show!* They live in their native Akron, Ohio, with their two sons, Craig and Wayne.

ABOUT THE ARTIST

Lisa Campbell Ernst grew up in Bartlesville, Oklahoma, and received her BFA in design from the University of Oklahoma. After working briefly for a New York advertising agency, she became a full-time free-lance artist and designer. Ms. Ernst and her husband Lee, an art director/designer, live in New York City, where they devote their spare time to collecting antiques, particularly children's toys, quilts and samplers.